Paul B. Du Chaillu

Lost in the jungle

Vol. 1

Paul B. Du Chaillu

Lost in the jungle
Vol. 1

ISBN/EAN: 9783337728595

Printed in Europe, USA, Canada, Australia, Japan

Cover: Foto ©ninafisch / pixelio.de

More available books at **www.hansebooks.com**

SHOOTING A LEOPARD. [p. 2.5.]

LOST IN THE JUNGLE.

NARRATED FOR YOUNG PEOPLE.

By PAUL DU CHAILLU,

AUTHOR OF

"DISCOVERIES IN EQUATORIAL AFRICA," "WILD LIFE UNDER THE EQUATOR," "JOURNEY TO ASHANGO LAND," "STORIES OF THE GORILLA COUNTRY," &c.

WITH NUMEROUS ENGRAVINGS.

NEW YORK:
HARPER & BROTHERS, PUBLISHERS,
FRANKLIN SQUARE.
1872.

CONTENTS.

CHAPTER I.
Paul's Letter to his Young Friends, in which he prepares them for being "Lost in the Jungle".................................Page 11

CHAPTER II.
A queer Canoe.—On the Rembo.—We reach the Niembouai.—A deserted Village.—Gazelle attacked by a Snake.—Etia wounded by a Gorilla.. 14

CHAPTER III.
Harpooning a Manga.—A great Prize.—Our Canoe capsized.—Description of the Manga.—Return to Camp................................ 23

CHAPTER IV.
We go into the Forest.—Hunt for Ebony-trees.—The Fish-eagles.—Capture of a young Eagle.—Impending Fight with them.—Fearful roars of Gorillas.—Gorillas breaking down Trees...................... 28

CHAPTER V.
Lost.—Querlaouen says we are Bewitched.—Monkeys and Parrots.—A deserted Village.—Strange Scene before an Idol.—Bringing in the Wounded.—An Invocation... 37

CHAPTER VI.
A white Gorilla.—Meeting two Gorillas.—The Female runs away.—The Man Gorilla shows fight.—He is killed.—His immense Hands and Feet.—Strange Story of a Leopard and a Turtle................. 48

CHAPTER VII.
Return to the Ovenga River.—The Monkeys and their Friends the Birds.—They live together.—Watch by Moonlight for Game.—Kill an Oshengui.. 55

CONTENTS.

CHAPTER VIII.

We are in a Canoe.—Outfit for Hunting.—See a beautiful Antelope.—Kill it.—It is a new Species.—River and forest Swallows..Page 62

CHAPTER IX.

We hear the Cry of a young Gorilla.—Start to capture him.—Fight with "his Father."—We kill him.—Kill the Mother.—Capture of the Baby.—Strange Camp Scene 70

CHAPTER X.

Jack will have his own way.—He seizes my Leg.—He tears my Pantaloons.—He growls at me.—He refuses cooked Food.—Jack makes his Bed.—Jack sleeps with one Eye open.—Jack is intractable. ... 81

CHAPTER XI.

Start after Land-crabs.—Village of the Crabs.—Each Crab knows his House.—Great flight of Crabs.—They bite hard.—Feast on the Slain.—A herd of Hippopotami 87

CHAPTER XII.

Strange Spiders.—The House-spider.—How they capture their Prey.—How they Fight.—Fight between a Wasp and a Spider.—The Spider has its Legs cut off, and is carried away.—Burrow Spider watching for its Prey... 94

CHAPTER XIII.

We continue our Wanderings.—Joined by Etia.—We starve.—Gambo and Etia go in search of Berries.—A herd of Elephants.—The rogue Elephant charges me.—He is killed.—He tumbles down near me.—Story of Redjioua... 106

CHAPTER XIV.

A formidable Bird.—The People are afraid of it.—A Baby carried off by the Guanionien.—A Monkey also seized.—I discover a Guanionien Nest.—I watch for the Eagles................................... 119

CHAPTER XV.

The Cascade of Niama-Biembai.—A native Camp.—Starting for the Hunt.—A Man attacked by a Gorilla.—His Gun broken.—The Man dies.—His Burial... 127

CHAPTER XVI.

Funeral of the Gorilla's Victim.—A Man's Head for the Alumbi.—The Snake and the Guinea-fowl.—Snake killed.—Visit to the House of the Alumbi.—Determine to visit the Sea-coast............ 137

CHAPTER XVII.

At Washington once more.—Delights of the Sea-shore.—I have been made a Makaga.—Friends object to my Return into the Jungle.—Quengueza taken Sick.—Gives a Letter to his Nephew.—Taking leave ....Page 142

CHAPTER XVIII.

Departure.—Arrival at Goumbi.—The People ask for the King.—A Death-panic in Goumbi.—A Doctor sent for.—Death to the Aniembas.—Three Women accused.—They are tried and killed....... 148

CHAPTER XIX.

Quengueza orders Ilogo to be consulted about his Illness.—What the People think of Ilogo.—A nocturnal Séance.—Song to Ilogo.—A female Medium.—What Ilogo said... 162

CHAPTER XX.

Departure from Goumbi.—Querlaouen's Village.—Find it deserted.—Querlaouen dead.—He has been killed by an Elephant.—Arrive at Obindji's Town.—Meeting with Querlaouen's Widow.—Neither Malaouen nor Gambo at home.................................. 167

CHAPTER XXI.

Leave for Ashira Land.—In a Swamp.—Cross the Mountains.—A Leopard after us.—Reach the Ashira Country....................... 175

CHAPTER XXII.

Great Mountains.—Ashira Land is beautiful.—The People are afraid.—Reach Akoonga's Village.—King Olenda sends Messengers and Presents.—I reach Olenda's Village................................ 181

CHAPTER XXIII.

King Olenda comes to receive me.—He is very old.—Never saw a Man so old before.—He beats his Kendo.—He salutes me with his Kombo.—Kings alone can wear the Kendo........................ 185

CHAPTER XXIV.

They all come to see me.—They say I have an Evil Eye.—Ashira Villages.—Olenda gives a great Ball in my Honor.—Beer-houses.—Goats coming out of a Mountain alive.................................. 190

CHAPTER XXV.

Ascension of the Ofoubou-Orèrè and Andelè Mountains.—The Ashiras bleed their Hands.—Story of a Fight between a Gorilla and a Leopard.—The Gorilla and the Elephant.—Wild Boars............ 197

CHAPTER XXVI.

Propose to start for Haunted Mountains.—Olenda says it can not be done.—At last I leave Olenda Village.—A Tornado.—We are Lost.—We fight a Gorilla.—We kill a Leopard.—Return to Olenda ....Page 203

CHAPTER XXVII.

Departure for the Apingi Country.—The Ovigui River.—Dangerous Bridge to Cross.—How the Bridge was built.—Glad to escape Drowning.—On the Way.—Reach the Oloumy......................... 217

CHAPTER XXVIII.

A Gorilla.—How he attacked me.—I kill him.—Minsho tells a Story of two Gorillas fighting.—We meet King Remandji.—I fall into an Elephant-pit.—Reach Apingi Land.. 226

CHAPTER XXIX.

First Day in Apingi Land.—I fire a Gun.—The Natives are Frightened.—I give the King a Waistcoat.—He wears it.—The Sapadi People.—The Music-box.—I must make a Mountain of Beads.... 238

CHAPTER XXX.

A large Fleet of Canoes.—We ascend the River.—The King paddles my Canoe.—Agobi's Village.—We upset.—The King is furious.—Okabi, the Charmer.—I read the Bible.—The People are afraid... 246

CHAPTER XXXI.

A great Crowd of Strangers.—I am made a King.—I remain in my Kingdom.—Good-by to the Young Folks...................................... 258

ILLUSTRATIONS.

	PAGE
SHOOTING A LEOPARD	*Frontispiece.*
THE ROYAL CANOE	15
THE MANGA	25
THE MPANO	29
FELLING EBONY-TREES	31
BRINGING IN THE WOUNDED	43
WATCHING BIRDS AND MONKEYS	57
SHOOTING THE NEW ANTELOPE	66
QUERLAOUEN AND HIS IDOL	78
CAUGHT BY JACK	82
GORILLA SLEEPING	85
CATCHING THE OGOMBONS	90
BIT BY A SPIDER	99
DEATH OF THE BULL ELEPHANT	111
GUANIONIEN CARRYING OFF A MONDI	122
GAMBO'S FRIEND KILLED BY A GORILLA	133
BIDDING GOOD-BY TO QUENGUEZA	147
"CHALLY, CHALLY, DO NOT LET ME DIE"	155
THE SONGS TO ILOGO	163
GIVING BEADS TO QUERLAOUEN'S WIFE	173
GOING TO ASHIRA LAND	177
RECEPTION OF THE KING OF THE ASHIRAS	186
THE KENDO	189
DRINKING PLANTAIN BEER	193
ATTACK ON THE WILD BOARS	201
AN ASHIRA IDOL	202
CROSSING THE OVIGUI RIVER	222
THE ELEPHANT-TRAP	233
THE MUSIC-BOX	243
OKABI AND THE LEOPARD	252
MY HOUSEKEEPER	256

LOST IN THE JUNGLE.

CHAPTER I.

PAUL'S LETTER TO HIS YOUNG FRIENDS, IN WHICH HE PREPARES THEM FOR BEING "LOST IN THE JUNGLE."

My dear Young Folks,—In the first book which I wrote for you, we traveled together through the Gorilla Country, and saw not only the gigantic apes, but also the cannibal tribes which eat men.

In the second book we continued our hunting, and met leopards, elephants, hippopotami, wild boars, great serpents, etc., etc. We were stung and chased by the fierce Bashikouay ants, and plagued by flies.

Last spring, your friend Paul, not satisfied with writing for young folks, took it into his head to lecture before them. When I mentioned the subject to my acquaintances, many of them laughed at the notion of my lecturing to you, and a few remarked, "This is another of your queer notions." I did not see it!!! I thought I would try.

Thousands of young folks came to your friend Paul's

lectures in Boston, Brooklyn, and New York; not only did my young friends come, but a great many old folks were also seen among them.

The intelligent, eager faces of his young hearers, their sparkling eyes, spoke to him more eloquently than words could do, and told him that he had done well to go into the great jungle of Equatorial Africa, and that they liked to hear what he had done and what he had seen.

When he asked the girls and boys of New York if he should write more books for them, the tremendous cheers and hurras they gave him in reply told him that he had better go to work.

When, at the end of his third lecture, he made his appearance in the old clothes he had worn in Africa, and said he would be happy to shake hands with his young hearers, the rush then made assured him that they were his friends. Oh! how your hearty hand-shaking gladdened the heart of your friend Paul; he felt so happy as your small hands passed in and out of his!

Before writing this new volume, I went to my good and esteemed friends, my publishers in Franklin Square, and asked them what they thought of a new book for Young Folks.

"Certainly," they said; "by all means, Friend Paul. Write a new book, for STORIES OF THE GORILLA COUNTRY and WILD LIFE UNDER THE EQUATOR are in great demand."

I immediately took hold of my old journals, removed the African dust from them, and went to work, and now we are going to be LOST IN THE JUNGLE.

There are countries and savages with which you have

been made acquainted in the two preceding volumes of which you will hear no more. Miengai, Ngolai, and Makinda are not to lead us through a country of cannibals. Aboko will slay no more elephants with me. Fasiko and Niamkala are to be left in their own country, and to many a great chief we have said good-by forever.

If we have left good friends and tribes of savage men, we will go into new countries and among other strange people. We shall have lots of adventures; we will slay more wild beasts, and will have fierce encounters with them, and some pretty narrow escapes. We will have some very hard times when "lost in the jungle;" we will be hungry and starving for many a day; we will see how curiously certain tribes live, what they eat and drink, how they build, and what they worship; and, before the end of our wanderings, you will see your friend Paul made KING over a strange people! It makes him laugh even now when he thinks of it.

I am sure we will not always like our life in the woods, but I hope, nevertheless, that you will not be sorry to have gone with me in the strange countries where I am now to lead you.

Let us get ready to start. Let us prepare our rifles, guns, and revolvers, and take with us a large quantity of shoes, quinine, powder, bullets, shot, and lots of beads and other things to make presents to the kings and people we shall meet. Oh dear, what loads! and every thing has to be carried on the backs of men! I shudder when I think of the trouble; but never mind; we shall get through our trials, sickness, and dangers safely. *En avant!* that is to say, forward!

CHAPTER II.

A QUEER CANOE.—ON THE REMBO.—WE REACH THE NIEMBOUAI.—A DESERTED VILLAGE.—GAZELLE ATTACKED BY A SNAKE.—ETIA WOUNDED BY A GORILLA.

The sun is hot; it is midday. The flies are plaguing us; the boco, the nchouna, the ibolai are hard at work, and the question is, which of these three flies will bite us the hardest; they feel lively, for they like this kind of weather, and they swarm round our canoes.

I wish you could have seen the magnificent canoes we had; they were made of single trunks of huge trees. We had left the village of Goumbi, where my good friend Quengueza, of whom I have spoken before, and the best friend I had in Africa, reigned.

Our canoes were paddling against the current of the narrow and deep River Rembo. You may well ask yourselves where is the place for which I am bound. If you had seen us you might have thought we were going to make war, for the canoes were full of men who were covered with all their war fetiches; their faces were painted, and they were loaded with implements of war. The drums beat furiously, and the paddlers, as we ascended, were singing war-songs, and at times they would sing praises in honor of their king, saying that Quengueza was above all kings.

Quengueza and I were in the royal canoe, a superb piece of wood over sixty feet long, the prow being an imitation of an immense crocodile's head, whose jaws were wide open, showing its big, sharp, pointed teeth. This was emblematic, and meant that it would swallow all the enemies of the king. In our canoe there were

THE ROYAL CANOE.

more than sixty paddlers. At the stern was seated old Quengueza, the queen, who held an umbrella over the head of his majesty, and myself, and seated back of us all was Adouma, the king's nephew, who was armed with an immense paddle, by which he guided the canoe.

How warm it was! Every few minutes I dipped my old Panama hat, which was full of green leaves, into the water, and also my umbrella, for, I tell you, the sun seemed almost as hot as fire. The bodies of the poor paddlers were shining with the oil that exuded from their skin.

If you had closely inspected our canoes you would have seen a great number of axes; also queer-looking harpoons, the use of which you might well be curious about. We were bound for a river or creek called the Niembouai, and on what I may call an African picnic; that is to say, we were going to build a camp on the banks of that river, and then we were to hunt wild beasts of the forest, but, above all, we were to try to harpoon an enormous creature called by the natives *manga*, a huge thing living in fresh water, and which one might imagine to be a kind of *whale*.

The distance from Goumbi to Niembouai was about fifteen miles. After three hours' paddling against a strong current we reached the Niembouai River. As we entered this stream the strong current ceased; the water became sluggish, and seemed to expand into a kind of lake, covered in many places with a queer kind of long tufted reed. For miles round the country looked entirely desolate. Now and then a flock of pelicans were seen swimming, and a long-legged crane was looking on the shore for fish.

At the mouth of the Niembouai, on a high hill, stood an abandoned Bakalai village called Akaka; the chief, whom I had known, was dead, and the people had fled for fear of the evil spirits. Nothing was left of the village but a few plantain-trees; the walls of the huts had all tumbled down.

How dreary all seemed for miles round Akaka. The

lands were overflowed, and, as I have said before, were covered with reeds. Far off against the sky, toward the east-northeast, towered high mountain peaks, which I hoped to explore. They rose blue against the sky, and seemed, as I looked at them through my telescope, to be covered with vegetation to their very tops. These mountains were the home of wild men and still wilder beasts. I thought at once how nice it would be for me to plant the Stars and Stripes on the highest mountains there.

As we advanced farther up the river the moun were lost sight of, and still we paddled up the N bouai. Canoe after canoe closed upon us, until a͏ͭ the whole fleet of King Quengueza were abreast o royal canoe, when I fired a gun, which was respond by a terrific yell from all the men.

Then Quengueza, with a loud voice, gave the order to make for a spot to which he pointed, where we were to land and build our camp. Soon afterward we reached the place, and found the land dry, covered with huge trees to protect us from the intense heat of the sun, from the heavy dews of night, and from slight showers.

The men all scattered into the forest, some to cut long poles and short sticks for our beds; others went to collect palm-leaves to make a kind of matting to be used as roofing. The first thing to be done was for the people to make a nice olako for their king and myself.

Our shelter was hardly finished when a terrible rainstorm burst upon us, preceded by a most terrific tornado, for we were in the month of March. By sunset the storm was all over; it cooled the air deliciously, for the heat had been intense. At noon, under the shade of my umbrella while in the canoe, the thermometer showed 119° Fahrenheit.

We had brought lots of food, and many women had accompanied us, who were to fish, and were also to cook for the people. The harpoons were well taken care of, for we fully expected to harpoon a few of the *mangas*.

The manga canoes were to arrive during the night, for the canoes we had were not fit for the capture of such large game.

In the evening old Quengueza was seated by the side of a bright fire; the good old man seemed quite happy. He had brought with him a jug of palm wine, from which he took a drink from time to time, until he began to feel the effects of the beverage, and became somewhat jolly. His subjects were clustered in groups around several huge fires, which blazed so brightly that the whole forest seemed to be lighted by them.

I put my two mats on my bed of leaves, hung my musquito nets as a protection against the swarms of musquitoes, then laid myself down under it with one of my guns at my side, placed my revolvers under my head, and bid good-night to Quengueza.

I did not intend to go right to sleep, but wished to listen to the talk of the people. The prospect of having plenty of meat to eat appeared to make them merry, and after each one had told his neighbor how much he could eat if he had it, and that he could eat more manga than any other man that he knew, the subject of food was exhausted. Then came stories of adventures with savage beasts and with ghosts.

We had in company many great men. The chief of them all was good old Quengueza, formerly a great w rior. After the king came Rapero Ouendogo, Azisha Olenga, Adouma, Rakenga Rikati Kombe, and Wombi —all men of courage and daring, belonging to the Abouya, a clan of warriors and hunters.

We had slaves also; among them many belonged to the king—slaves that loved him, and whose courage was as great as that of any man belonging to the tribe. Among them was Etia, the mighty and great slayer of gorillas and elephants. Etia provided game for Quengueza's table; he was one of the beloved slaves of the king, and he was also a great friend of mine. We were, indeed, old friends, for we had hunted a good deal together.

On a sudden all merriment stopped, for Ouendogo had shouted "let Etia tell us some of his hunting adventures." This order was received with a tremendous cheer, and Etia was placed in the centre. How eager were the eyes and looks of those who knew the story-telling gift of their friend Etia, who began thus: "Years ago, I remember it as well as if it were but yesterday, I was in a great forest at the foot of a high hill, through which a little stream was murmuring; the jungle was dense, so much so that I could hardly see a few steps ahead of me; I was walking carefully along, very carefully, for I was hunting after the gorilla, and I had already met with the footprints of a huge one. I looked on the right, on the left, and ahead of me, and I wished I had had four eyes, that is, two more eyes on the back of my head, for I was afraid that a great gorilla might spring upon me from behind."

We all got so impatient to hear the story that we shouted all at once, "Go on, Etia, go on. What did you see in the bush? Tell us quick." But Etia was not to be hurried faster than he chose. After a short pause, he continued: "I do not know why, but a feeling of fear crept over me. I had a presentiment that something queer was going to happen. I stood still and looked all round me.

"Suddenly I spied a huge python coiled round a tree near to a little brook. The serpent was perfectly quiet. His huge body was coiled several times round the tree close to the ground, and there he was waiting for animals to come and drink. It was the dry season, and water was very scarce, and many animals came to that spring to drink. I can see, even to this day, its glittering eyes. Its color was almost identical with that of the bark of the tree. I immediately lay down behind another tree, for I had come also in search of game, and I could do nothing better than wait for the beasts to come there and drink.

"Ere long I spied a ncheri 'gazelle' coming; she approached unsuspicious of any danger. Just as she was in the act of drinking, the snake sprang upon the little beast and coiled himself round it. For a short time there was a desperate struggle; the folds of the snake became tighter and tighter round the body of the poor animal. I could see how slowly, but how surely the snake was squeezing its prey to death. A few smothered cries, and all was over; the animal was dead. Then the snake left the tree and began to swallow the gazelle, commencing at the head. It crushed the animal more and more in its folds. I could hear the bones crack, and I could see the animal gradually disappearing down the throat of the snake."

"Why did you not, Etia, kill the snake at once?" shouted one man, "and then you would have had the ncheri for your dinner?" "Wait," replied Etia.

"After I had watched the snake for a short time, I took my cutlass and cut the big creature to pieces. That night I slept near the spot. I lighted a big fire, cooked a piece of the snake for my meal, and went to sleep.

"The next morning I started early, and went off to hunt. I had not been long in the forest before I heard a noise; it was a gorilla. I immediately got my gun ready, and moved forward to meet him. I crept through the jungle flat on 'my belly,' and soon I could see the great beast tearing down the lower branches of a tree loaded with fruit. Suddenly he stopped, and I shouted to him, 'Kombo (male gorilla), come here! come here!' He turned round and gave a terrific yell or roar, his fierce, glaring eyes looked toward me, he raised his big long arms as if to lay hold of me, and then advanced. We were very near, for I had approached quite close before I shouted my defiance to him.

"When he was almost touching me, I leveled my gun —that gun which my father, King Quengueza, had given me—that gun for which I have made a fetich, and which never misses an animal—then I fired. The big beast tottered, and, as it fell, one of his big hands got hold of one of my legs; his big, thick, huge fingers, as he gave his death-gasp, contracted themselves; I gave a great cry of pain, and, seizing my battle-axe, I dealt a fearful stroke and broke its arm just above the joint. But his fingers and nails had gone deep into my flesh, which it lacerated and tore."

Etia pointed to his leg, and continued: "I have never gotten over it to this day, though it is so long ago that very few of you that are here to-night were born then. I began to bleed and bleed, and feared that the bone of my leg was broken. I left the body of the gorilla in the woods, but took its head with me, and that head I have still in my plantation; and at times," added Etia, "its jaws open during the night, and it roars and says, 'Etia, why have you killed me?' I am sure that gorilla had been a man before. That is the reason I am lame to this day. I succeeded in reaching my pindi (plantation), and my wife took care of me; but from that day I have hated gorillas, and I have vowed that I would kill as many of them as I could."

The story of Etia had the effect of awakening every one. They all shouted that Etia is a great hunter, that Etia had been bewitched before he started that time, and that if it had not been for Etia having a powerful monda (fetich), he would have been killed by the gorilla.

Our story-telling was interrupted by the arrival of canoes, just built for the fishing of the manga. These canoes were unlike other canoes; they were flat-bottomed, as flat as a board; the sides were straight, and both ends were sharp-pointed, and, when loaded with two men, did not draw in the water, I am sure, half an inch. They glided over the water, causing scarcely a ripple. There was no seat, and a man had to paddle standing up, the paddle being almost as long as a man. These canoes were about twenty-five feet long, and from eighteen to twenty inches broad. In them were several queer kinds of harpoons, which were to be used in capturing the mangas.

CHAPTER III.

HARPOONING A MANGA.— A GREAT PRIZE. — OUR CA[NOE] CAPSIZED. — DESCRIPTION OF THE MANGA. — RETURN [TO] CAMP.

The next morning, very early, if you had been on [the] banks of the Niembouai, you would have seen me on [one] of those long flat-bottomed canoes which I have descr[ibed] to you, and in it you would likewise have seen two manga harpoons.

A man by the name of Ratenou, who had the re[puta]tion of being one of the best manga harpooners, a[nd] knowing where they were to be found, was with me. [He] was covered with fetiches, and had in a pot a large [quan]tity of leaves of a certain shrub, which had been m[ixed] with water and then dried. This mixture, when [scat]tered on the water, is said to attract the manga.

When we left the shore, being less of an expert [than] Ratenou, and not being able to stand up so easily a[s he] did, I seated myself at the bottom of the canoe. R[ate]nou recommended me not to move at all, and while [he] paddled I could not even hear the dip of his paddl[e in] the water, so gently did our boat glide along.

We crossed the Niembouai to the opposite shore, wh[ere] we lay by among the reeds. By that time the twili[ght] had just made its appearance, and you know the twili[ght] is of short duration under the equator; indeed, there is hardly any at all.

Ratenou threw on the water, not far from where we lay in watch, some of the green stuff he had in the pot, and we had not waited long before I saw, coming along the surface of the water, a huge beast, which gave two or three puffs and then disappeared. My man watched intently, and in the mean time moved the canoe toward the spot. We came from behind, so that the animal could not see us, and, just as the manga came to the surface of the water once more, and gave three gentle puffs, Ratenou sent the harpoon with tremendous force into his body. The huge creature, with a furious dash and jerk at the line, made for the bottom of the river. Ratenou let the line slip, but held back as much as he dared, in order thus to increase the pain inflicted on the beast. The suspense and excitement were great. The animal dashed down to the bottom with impetuous haste, but the harpoon was fast in him, and held him. We watched the rope going out with the utmost anxiety. The harpoon has hardly struck the manga when our canoe goes with fearful rapidity. The native's rope proved too short; there was not enough of it to let it go. Every moment I fully expected to upset, and did not relish the idea at all. Finally the rope slackened; the manga was getting exhausted. At last no strain was observable; the beast was dead. Without apparently much effort, the line was hauled in, and presently I saw the huge beast alongside the canoe.

"Let us upset the canoe," said Ratenou.

"What!" said I.

"Let us upset the canoe." The good fellow, who was

not overloaded with clothes, thought that to be an easy task; but I did not look at the proposal quite in the same light; so I said, "Ratenou, let us paddle the canoe to the shore, and I will get out." It was hardly said before it was done. I landed, and then the huge manga was tied to the canoe, the latter was capsized over its back, and then we turned it over again.

This was a big prize, for there is no meat so much thought of among the savages as that of the manga. We immediately made for the camp, and were received with uproarious cheers.

The canoe was upset once more, and the big freshwater monster was dragged ashore. It was hard work, for the huge beast must have weighed from fifteen to eighteen hundred pounds.

THE MANGA.

What a queer-looking thing it was! The manga is a new species of manatee. Its body is of a dark lead-color; the skin is very thick and smooth, and covered in all parts with single bristly hairs, from half an inch to an

B

inch in length; but the hairs are at a distance from each other, so that the skin appears almost smooth. The eyes are small—very small; it has a queer-looking head, the upper and lower parts of the lips having very hard and bristly hair.

The manga is unlike the whale in this, that it has two paddles, which are used as hands; and, when the flesh or skin is removed, the skeleton of the paddles looks very much like the bony frame of a hand. I have named this curious species after my most esteemed friend, Professor Owen, of London, *Manatus Oweni*.

The skin of the manga, when dried, is of a most beautiful amber color; the nearer the middle of the back, the more beautiful and intense the yellow. The skin is there more than one inch in thickness. When fresh it has a milky color, but when it dries, and the water goes off, it turns yellow. That part of the back is carefully cut in strips by the natives, who make whips with it, just in the same way as they do with the hippopotamus hide, and these whips are used extensively on the backs of their wives.

The large, broad tail, which is shown in the engraving, is used by them as a rudder, while their hands are used as paddles. These hands, unlike those of seals, have no claws or nails. This manga was eleven feet long, and the body looked quite huge.

Mangas feed entirely on grass and the leaves of trees, the branches of which fall into the water; they feed, also, on the grass found at the bottom of the rivers.

In looking at such curious shaped things, I could not help thinking what queer animals were found on our globe.

The doctor was greatly rejoiced at our success. Then came the ceremony of cutting up the beast; but, before commencing, Ratenon, the manga doctor, went through some ceremony round the carcase which he did not want any one to see. After a little he began to cut up the meat.

It was very fat; on the stomach the fat must have been about two inches thick. The lean meat was white, with a reddish tinge, and looked very nice. It is delicious, something like pork, but finer grained and of sweeter flavor. It must be smoked for a few days in order to have it in perfection.

We cut the body into pieces of about half a pound each, and put them on the oralas and smoked Master Manga. The fragrance filled our camp.

The manga belongs to the small but singular group of animals classed as SIRENIA.

I have often watched these manga feeding on the leaves of trees, the branches of which hung close to the water. The manga's head only shows above the water. When thus seen, the manga bears a curious resemblance to a human being. They never go ashore, and do not crawl even partly out of the water. They must sometimes weigh as much as two to three thousand pounds.

CHAPTER IV.

WE GO INTO THE FOREST.—HUNT FOR EBONY-TREES.—THE FISH-EAGLES.—CAPTURE OF A YOUNG EAGLE.—IMPENDING FIGHT WITH THEM.—FEARFUL ROARS OF GORILLAS.—GORILLAS BREAKING DOWN TREES.

SEVERAL weeks have passed since we left the Niembouai. I have been alone with my three great hunters, Querlaouen, Gambo, and Malaouen. We are sworn friends; we have resolved to live in the woods and to wander through them. Several times since we left our manga-fishing we have been "lost in the jungle."

We have had some very hard times, but splendid hunting; and on the evening of that day of which I speak, we were quietly seated somewhere near the left bank of the River Ovenga, by the side of a bright fire, and, at the same time my men enjoyed their smoke, we talked over the future prospects of our life in the forest.

That evening I said, "Boys, let us go into the forest and look for ebony-trees; I want to find them; I must take some of that wood with me when I go back to the land of 'the spirits.'" Malouen, Gambo, and Querlaouen shouted at once, "Let us go in search of the ebony-tree; let us choose a spot where we shall be able to find game." For I must tell you that good eating was one of the weak points of my three friends.

The ebony-tree is scattered through the forest in clusters. It is one of the finest and most graceful among the many lovely trees that adorn the African forest. Its leaves are long, sharp-pointed, and of a dark green color. Its bark is smooth, and also a dark green. The trunk rises straight as an arrow. Queer to say, the ebony-tree, when old, becomes hollow, and even some of its branches are hollow. Next to the bark is a white "sap-wood." Generally that sap-wood is three or four inches thick; so, unless one knows the tree by the bark, the first few blows of an axe would not reveal to him the dark, black wood found inside. Young ebony-trees of two feet diameter are often perfectly white; then, as the tree grows bigger, the black part is streaked with the white, and as the tree matures, the black predominates, and eventually takes the place of the white. The wood of the ebony-tree is very hard; the grain short and very brittle.

You can see that it is no slight work to cut down such big trees with the small axes we had, such as represented in the accompanying drawing. I show you, also, the

drawing of a mpano, which is the instrument used in hollowing out the trunks of trees to make canoes.

After wandering for some hours we found several ebony-trees. How beautiful they were, and how graceful was the shape of their sharp-pointed leaves! These trees were not very far from the river, or I should rather say from a creek which fell into the Ovenga River, so that it would not be difficult to carry our ebony logs to the banks and there load them on canoes.

We immediately went to work and built a nice camp. We had with us two boys, Njali and Nola, who had been sent with a canoe laden with provisions from one of Querlaouen's plantations, and which his wife had forwarded to us. Some bunches of plantains were of enormous size. There were two bunches of bananas for me, and sundry baskets of cassava and peanuts. There was also a little parcel of dried fish, which Querlaouen's wife had sent specially to her friend Chally.

We set to work, and soon succeeded in felling two ebony-trees. We arranged to go hunting in the morning, and cut the wood into billets in the afternoon. As we were not in a hurry, and it was rather hard work, we determined to take our time.

By the side of our camp we had a beautiful little stream, where we obtained our drinking water, and a little below that spot there was a charming place where we could take a bath.

Not far from our camp there was a creek called Eliva Mono (the Mullet's Creek), so named on account of the great number of mullets which at a certain season of the year come there to spawn. Besides the mono, the creek contained great numbers of a fish called condo. Large and tall trees grew on the banks of the creek.

FELLING EBONY-TREES.

This creek was at that time of the year a resort for the large fish-eagles. These birds could look down from the tops of the high trees, on which they perched, upon the water below, and watch for their finny prey.

The waters of the creek were so quiet that half the time not a ripple could be seen on them. High up on some of the trees could be seen the nests belonging to these birds of prey.

There were several eagles, and they belonged to two different species. One was called by the natives *coungou*, and was known all over the country, for it is found as far as the sea. Its body was white, and of the size of a fowl, and it had black wings, the spread of which was very great, and the birds were armed with thick and strong talons. The females were of a gray color.

Another eagle was also found on the creek. It was a larger bird, of dark color, and called by the natives the compagnondo (*Tephrodornis ocreatus*). The shrill cries of this bird could be heard at a great distance, sounding strangely in the midst of the great solitude. Both these eagles feed on fish, and two of the coungous had their nest on the top of a very high tree, and in that nest there were young ones. The nest was built, like most of the fish-eagles' nests, with sticks of trees, and occupied a space of several feet in diameter. When once the nest is built it is occupied a good number of years in succession. It is generally placed between the forks of the branches, and can be seen at a great distance. Each year the nest requires repairs, which both the male and female birds attend to. These coungous seemed very much attached to each other. After one of a pair had been shot, I would hear the solitary one calling for its mate, and it would remain day after day near the spot, and at last would either take another mate or fly off to another country. When a pair of coungous, male and female, were killed, then the next year another couple would take possession of their nest.

I often watched the coungous' nest. They were always on the look-out for fish. Now and then they would dive and seize a fine mullet, which they would carry up to their young and feed them. How quick they were in their motion! Sometimes one would catch a fish so big and heavy that it seemed hardly strong enough to rise in the air with it. The natives say that sometimes the eagles are carried under the water when they have caught a fish too big for their strength, and from whose body they can not extricate their firmly-fixed talons before the fish dives to the bottom.

When the old birds approached the nest with food the young ones became very noisy, evincing their impatience for the treat of fresh fish, with which the parents sometimes hovered over the nest as if desirous of tantalizing their appetite.

One day I took it into my head to have the tree cut down, so that I could examine the nest. The old birds were greatly excited, for they saw that something was wrong. At last the tree fell with a great crash. I immediately made for the nest, and I can not tell you what a stench arose from it; it was fearful. Remnants of decayed fish and many other kinds of offal made a smell which it was surprising the young eagles could endure. In the mean time the young ones had tumbled out of the nest, and while we were looking for them, and just after I had captured one, the parents came swooping down. Goodness! I thought I was going to be attacked by them, for they hovered round, sometimes coming quite close to me; once or twice I thought my hat at least would be carried off. Becoming worried, I raised my gun and fired, and killed the male; then the female got frightened and flew away. The young were covered with gray down. They must certainly possess very limited powers of smell, for I can not see how any living thing could exist in the midst of such odors.

On one of my excursions up the creek I discovered another coungou nest, and, as it was not built in a very high tree, I determined to examine its economy. So, with pretty hard work, I climbed up another tree, from whence, with the aid of my field-telescope, I could watch all that went on in the nest, which contained two young eagles. During the first few days the old birds would feed their young by tearing the flesh of the fish with their beaks, while their talons held it fast. When the coungous are young, the male and female have the same gray plumage, which in the male turns white and black when old.

One fine afternoon I left the camp all alone, Gambo, Malaouen, and Querlaouen being fast asleep. Before I knew it, I found myself far away, for I had been thinking of home and of friends, and, walking in a good hunting path, I had gone farther than I thought, and time had fled pleasantly. I carried on my shoulder a double-barrel, smooth-bore gun, intending to take a short walk in the woods. When I looked at my watch, it was 2 o'clock! I had been gone three hours. Just as I was ready to turn back, I thought I heard distant thunder. I listened attentively, and I perceived that the noise was not thunder, but the terrific roar of a gorilla at some distance. Though it was getting late, I thought I would go in that direction; so I took out the small shot with which one of the barrels of my gun was loaded, and put in a heavy bullet instead. My revolvers were in the belt round my waist, and had been loaded that very morning. As I approached the spot where the beast was, the more awful sounded the roar, till at last the whole forest re-echoed with the din, and appeared to shake with the tremendous voice of the animal. It was awful; it was appalling to hear. What lungs the monster had, to enable him to emit so deep and awe-inspiring a noise. The other inhabitants of the forest seemed to be silent; the few birds that were in it had stopped their warbling. Suddenly I heard a crash—two crashes. The animal was in the act of breaking the limbs of trees. Then the noise of the breaking of trees ceased, and the roar of the monster recommenced. This time it was answered by a weaker roar. The echoes swelled and died away from hill to hill, and the whole forest was filled with the din. The man gorilla and his wife were talking together: they no doubt understood each other, but I could not hear any articulate sound. I stopped and examined my gun. Just as I got ready to enter the jungle from the hunting-path to go after the male gorilla, the roaring ceased. I waited for its renewal, but the silence of the forest was no more to be disturbed that day.

After waiting half an hour I hurried back toward the camp. I walked as fast as I could, for I was afraid that darkness would overtake me. Six o'clock found me in the woods; the sun had just set, and the short twilight of the equator which followed the setting of the sun warned me to hurry faster than ever if I wanted to reach the camp. Hark! I hear voices. What can these voices be, those of friends or enemies? I moved from the hunting-path and ascended an adjacent tree, but soon I heard voices that I recognized as those of Malaouen and

Querlaouen shouting "Moguizi, where are you? Moguizi, where are you?" I responded "I am coming! I am coming!" and soon after they gave a tremendous hurrah; we had met.

We soon reached the camp, and I rested my weary limbs by the side of a blazing fire and dried my clothes, which were quite wet, for I had crossed several little streams.

CHAPTER V.

LOST.—QUERLAOUEN SAYS WE ARE BEWITCHED.—MONKEYS AND PARROTS.—A DESERTED VILLAGE.—STRANGE SCENE BEFORE AN IDOL.—BRINGING IN THE WOUNDED.—AN INVOCATION.

We soon after left the left bank of the Ovenga and crossed over to the other side, but not before having carefully stored under shelter the billets of ebony-wood we had taken so much pains to cut, and which I wanted to take home with me.

The country where we now were was very wild, and seemed entirely uninhabited. At any rate, we did not know of any people or village for miles round.

After wandering for many, many days through the forest, we came suddenly on a path. Immediately Querlaouen, Gambo, Malaouen, and I held a great council, and, in order not to be heard in case some one might pass, we went back half a mile farther from the path in the forest. Then we seated ourselves, and began to speak in a low voice.

Querlaouen spoke first, and said that he did not know the country, and could not tell what we had better do, except that every one should have his gun ready, and his powder and bullets handy, his eyes wide open, and his ears ready to catch even the sound of a falling leaf or the footsteps of a gazelle.

Gambo said Querlaouen was right.

Then Malouen rose and said: "For days we have been in these woods, and we have seen no living being, no path; we have fed on wild honey, on berries, nuts, and fruits, and to-day we have at last come upon a path. We know that the path has been made by some people or other. It is true we know that we are in the Ashankolo Mountains; that the tribe of Bakalai, living there, are a fighting people; but," he said, "he thought it was better to go back and follow the path until we came to the place where the people lived."

Querlaouen got up and said: "We have been lost in this forest, and, though we look all round us, there is not a tree we recognize; the little streams we pass we know not. The ant-hills we have seen are not the same as those in our own country. The large stones are not of the shape of the stones we are accustomed to look upon. We must have been bewitched before we left the village."

This suggestion of friend Querlaouen was received by a cheer from my two other fellows, I being the only one that did not believe in what he said.

"For," continued he, "this has never happened to us before. Yes, somebody wants to bewitch us."

While he thus talked, his gentle and amiable face assumed a fierce expression, and the other two said "Yes, somebody wants to bewitch us; but he had better look out, for surely he will die."

At last I said, "Let us get back to the path, and follow it; perhaps we will meet some strange adventure."

Just as we rose to move on we heard the chatter of

monkeys, and we made for the spot whence the sound proceeded, in the hope that we might kill one or two. Carefully we went through the jungle, the prospect of killing a monkey filling our hearts with joy; for we could already, in anticipation, see a bright fire blazing, and some part of a monkey boiling in the little iron pot we carried with us; for myself, I imagined a nice piece roasting on a bright charcoal fire.

At last we came to the foot of a very high tree, and, raising our heads, we could see several monkeys. The tree was so tremendously high that the monkeys hardly appeared larger than squirrels. How could our small shot reach the top of that tree, which was covered with red berries, upon which the monkeys were quietly feeding? Although we could not reach them, they were not to be left in undisturbed possession, for a large flock of gray parrots, with red tails, flew round and round the tree, screeching angry defiance at the monkeys, who had at first been hidden by the thick leaves. The monkeys screamed back fierce menaces, running out on the slender branches in vain endeavor to catch their feathered opponents, who would fly off, only to return with still more angry cries. Both parrots and monkeys being out of reach of our guns, we were obliged to leave them to settle the right of possession to the rich red fruit.

How weary we were when we struck the path again! and, having first passed a field of plantain-trees, we at last arrived at a village.

Not a living creature was to be seen in it. Not even a goat, a fowl, or a dog, although we found several fires smouldering, from which the smoke still ascended. We proceeded carefully, for we did not know what kind of people inhabited this village. But I said, "Boys, let us go straight through the place."

So we went on until we came to an ouandja (a building), where, in a dark corner of a room, stood a huge image of an idol. Oh! how ugly it was. It represented a woman with a wide-open mouth, through which protruded a long, sharp-pointed iron tongue.

At the foot of the idol we found the skulls of all kinds of animals, elephants, leopards, hyenas, monkeys, and squirrels—even of crocodiles; and skins of snakes, intermingled with bunches of dry, queer-looking leaves, the ashes of burnt bones, and the shells of huge land turtles.

How horribly strange the big idol looked in the corner! It made me shudder.

The village was deserted, darkness was coming on, and the question now was, What were we going to do? Should we sleep in that forlorn-looking village or not? If we staid there the villagers might return when we were asleep.

For some time we regarded each other in silence; then I said, "Boys, I think we had better sleep in the forest, away from the path, but not far from the village." Gambo, Malouen, and Querlaouen shouted with one voice, "That is so. Let us sleep in the forest, for this village seems to us full of aniemba (witchcraft)."

So we returned to the jungle, and collected large leaves to be used for roofing a hut which was quickly built with limbs from dead trees that lay scattered about, yielding also a plentiful supply of wood for a rousing fire. When every thing was ready, I pulled my match-box from my bag and lighted our fire.

Night came, and all life seemed to go to rest. Now and then I could hear the cry of some wild night animal, which had left his lair in search of prey, and was calling for its mate.

Before midnight we were aroused by the muttering of distant thunder; a tornado was coming. The trees began to shake violently, the wind became terrific; soon we heard the branches of trees breaking; then the trees themselves began to fall, and with such a crash as to alarm us greatly. Suddenly, not far from our hut, one of the big giant trees of the forest came down with a fearful noise, and crushing in its mighty fall dozens of other trees, one of them adjoining our camp. We got up in the twinkle of an eye, frightened out of our wits, for we fancied the whole forest was going to tumble down. The monkeys chattered; a terrific roar from a gorilla resounded through the forest, mingling with the howls of hyenas. Snakes, no doubt, were crawling about. Immediately after the falling of the great tree near us we heard a novel and tremendous noise in the jungle, coming from a herd of elephants fleeing in dismay, and breaking down every thing in their path.

"Goodness gracious!" I shouted, in English, "what does all this mean? Are we going to be buried alive in the forest?" The words were scarcely out of my mouth when there came a blinding flash of lightning, instantaneously followed by a peal of thunder like a volley from a hundred cannon, that seemed to shake the very earth to its foundation; and then the rain fell in torrents, and soon deluged the ground. Happily, we knew what we were about when we built our fires, for we had started them on the top of large logs of wood, so arranged that it would have required more than a foot of water on the ground before it could reach the fires and extinguish them. Then our leaves were so broad and nicely arranged that they entirely protected us from the storm, and our shelter was perfected by the branches of the great tree which, in falling, had apparently threatened our destruction.

The terrible hubbub lasted some hours, the continued lightning and thunder preventing sleep; but toward 4 o'clock in the morning the storm ceased, and all again became quiet; only the dripping of the water from the leaves could be heard; then we went to sleep, but not before having arranged our fires in such a manner that we could go to rest in comparative safety.

In the early morning, before dawn, and while we were only half awake, I thought I heard the sound of a human voice. Listen! We all listened attentively, and Gambo laid down with his ears to the ground, and then he declared that he distinctly heard voices in the direction of the village. There was no doubt—the people had returned.

"Let us go," said I, "and find out what kind of neighbors these are. We have our guns and plenty of ammunition, so we need not fear them; but let us act with caution."

This was agreed to. So, leaving our camp, we quietly crept near the village, until we gained a spot from whence we could see all that was going on. Men with lighted torches were entering the village, and four of them bore what, to all appearances, was a dead body, which they deposited before the huge idol, now moved out into the open street. The gleam of the torches re-

BRINGING IN THE WOUNDED.

vealed to us that this prostrate body had been pierced by many spears, part of which still remained in it.

Every man was armed to the teeth, but not a woman was visible. The scene was strange and wild. Not a word was uttered after the body of the wounded man had been laid on the ground. How strange and wild the men looked by the lurid glare of their torches! Their bodies were painted and covered with fetiches. Just back of the huts stood the tall trees, whose branches moved to and fro in the wind. I could hear its whispers as it passed through the foliage of the trees. The stars were shining beautifully, and a few fleecy white clouds were floating above our heads. I wish you could have seen us as we lay flat on the ground. Our eyes must have been bright indeed as we looked on the wild scene; and this I know, that our hearts were beating strongly as we lay close together. If, perchance, one of us had been seized with a fit of sneezing, or a fit of coughing, it might have been the end of us, for the savages would have been alarmed, and, believing us to be enemies, would at once have attacked us; so we had started on a rather risky business. I had never thought of it before; it was always so with me at that time. I thought of the danger after I was in it.

Soon another batch of men made their appearance, carrying another wounded man, who appeared almost dead, and they laid him by the side of the other, and then the women came in, carrying their babies and leading their children.

There stood the huge idol looking grimly at the scene. How ugly it seemed, with its copper eyes and wide-open mouth, which showed two rows of sharp-pointed teeth!

In one of its hands it held a sharp-pointed knife, and in the other it held a bearded spear. It had a necklace of leopards' teeth, and its hideous head was decorated with birds' feathers. One side of its face was painted yellow, the other white; the forehead was painted red, and a black stripe did duty for eyebrows. I could not make out whether it represented a male or a female.

By its side stood the people, as silent as the idol itself.

At last a man came in front of the idol, and at once, by the language he spoke in, we knew him to be a Bakalai.

"Mbuiti," he said, addressing the idol, "we have been to the war, and now we have returned. There lie before thee two of our number; look at them. You see the spear-wounds that have gone into their bodies. They can not talk. When they were strong they went to the jungle and shot game, and when they had killed it they always brought some to give thee; many times they have brought to thee antelopes, wild boars, and other wild beasts. They have brought thee sugar-cane, ground-nuts, plantains, and bananas; they have given thee palm wine to drink. Oh, Mbuiti, do thou heal them!" And all the people shouted "Do make them well." How queer their voices resounded in the forest!

Suddenly, all the torches were extinguished, and the village was again in darkness. Not a voice was heard; complete silence followed. They were evidently afraid of an attack, and retired quietly to their huts.

I was very glad that we had managed to see all this without having been discovered; we did not think it safe, however, to move away before giving the villagers time to fall asleep, and then we realized new causes for apprehension. It was not a very pleasant or safe thing to be out in this jungle in the early morning before it was light. We might tread on a snake, or lay hold of one folded among the lower branches of the trees on which we laid our hands; or a wandering leopard might be prowling round; and, as there certainly were gorillas in the neighborhood, we might come on a tree which a female gorilla with a baby had climbed into for the night, and then we should have the old fellow upon us showing fight. I confess I did not care to fight gorillas in the dark. Again, a party of Bashikouay might be encountered, when nothing would be left for us but flight.

After our breakfast of nuts and berries, the question naturally arose, Shall we go back to the strange village? "Certainly not," at once said Querlaouen; "we do not know what kind of Bakalai they are."

When my turn to speak came, I said, "Boys, why not go and learn from these people the causes which led to their affray, and at the same time learn exactly in what part of the forest we are?"

For about a minute we were all silent. My three savages were thinking about my proposal; then Malaouen said, "Chaillie, we had better not go. Who knows? it may be that the wounded men we saw the people bringing into the village were found speared in the path, and, if so, we might be suspected of being the men who speared them. Then," said he, "what a palaver we should get in! and there would be no other way for us to get out of our troubles except by fighting. You know that the Bakalai here fight well." We all gave our assent to Malaouen's wise talk, for I must tell you, boys, my three men had good common sense, and many a time have I listened to their counsels. "Besides, we have a good deal of hunting to do," said Malaouen, "and we had better attend to it."

"Yes," we all said, with one voice. "Let us attend to our hunting. Let us have a jolly good time in the woods, and kill as many gorillas, elephants, leopards, antelopes, wild boars, and other wild beasts as we can." It being settled we should not go back to the village, we all got up, looked at our guns carefully, and plunged into the woods once more.

If you could have seen us, you would have said, What wild kind of chaps these four fellows are! Indeed we did look wild. We did not mind it; our hearts were bound together, we were such great friends. I am sure many of you who read these pages would have been our friends also, if you had been there.

CHAPTER VI.

A WHITE GORILLA.—MEETING TWO GORILLAS.—THE FEMALE RUNS AWAY.—THE MAN GORILLA SHOWS FIGHT.—HE IS KILLED.—HIS IMMENSE HANDS AND FEET.—STRANGE STORY OF A LEOPARD AND A TURTLE.

SOME time has elapsed since that strange night-scene I have described to you in the preceding chapter. We had gone, as you are aware, into the woods hunting for wild game. All I can say is, that I wish some of you had been with us. We had a glorious time! lots of fun, and cleared that part of the forest of the few wild beasts that were in it: one elephant, one gorilla, three antelopes, two wild boars were killed, besides smaller game, and some queer-looking birds. Once or twice we had pretty narrow escapes.

I wish you had been with us to enjoy the thunder and lightning. It would have given you an idea of the noise the thunder can make, and the brightness a flash of lightning can attain; how heavy the rain can fall; and a tornado would have shown you how strong the wind can blow. For the thunder we hear and the rains that fall at home can not give us any conception of what takes place in the mountainous and woody regions of Equatorial Africa. After all, there is some enjoyment in being "lost in the jungle" in the country in which I have taken you to travel with me.

Once more I am in sight of the Ovenga. For some time the people inhabiting the banks of that river had whispered among themselves that a white gorilla had been seen. At first the story of a white gorilla was believed in by only a few, but at last the white gorilla's appearance was the talk of every body. Gambo, Querlaouen, and Malaouen were firm believers in it.

Both men and women would come back to their villages and assure the people that they had had a glimpse of the creature. He looked so old he could hardly walk. His hair was perfectly white, and he was terribly wrinkled. He must have lived forever in the forest, and was, no doubt, the great-grandfather of hundreds of gorillas. His wife must have died long ago. He was a monster in size. Then old men said they remembered, when they were boys, that a man disappeared from the village; perhaps he had been caught by that very gorilla.

"How is it," said I to the people, "that I have never seen a white gorilla?" They would answer, "There are white-headed men, so there are white-haired gorillas. A white gorilla is not often to be seen, for when he becomes so old that he turns white, he lives quite alone, and in a part of the forest where people can not go, for the jungle is too thick there. He seems to be too knowing, and keeps out of the way of the hunting-path." "Of course," they would add, "its skin remains black."

Day after day we went through the forest to see if we could get a glimpse of the white gorilla. We had been a whole week in quest of the white gorilla, never camping twice in the same spot; often Malaouen and Querlaouen declared that they would go and hunt alone, while Gambo and I, with a boy we had with us, should

C

choose our own course, always appointing a certain place near a hunting-path where we could all meet at sunset.

On the last day of the week, we had been on the hunt for several hours, when we came upon tolerably fresh tracks of a gorilla; judging by the immense footprints he had left on the ground, he must be a monster—a tremendous big fellow. Was he a white gorilla or not? These tracks we followed cautiously, and at last, in a densely-wooded and quite dark ravine, we came suddenly upon two gorillas, a male and a female. The old man gorilla was by the side of his wife, fondly regarding her. They had no baby. How dark and horrid their intensely black faces appeared! I watched them for a few minutes, for, thanks to the dense jungle in which we were concealed, I was not perceived at once. But, on a sudden, the female uttered a cry of alarm, and ran off before we could get a shot at her, being lost to sight in a moment. We were not in a hurry to fire at her. Of course the male must be killed first; it is ten times safer to get him out of the way.

The male had no idea of running off. As soon as the female disappeared, he gazed all round with his savage-looking eyes. He then rose slowly from his haunches, and at once faced us, uttering a roar of rage at our evidently untimely intrusion, coming as we had to disturb him and frighten his wife, when they were quietly seated side by side. Gambo and I were accompanied by the boy, who carried our provisions and an extra gun, a double-barrel smooth bore. The boy fell to the rear of us, and we stood side by side and awaited the advance of the hideous monster. In the dim half-light of the ravine, his features working with rage; his gloomy, treacherous, mischievous gray eyes; his rapidly-agitated and frightful, satyr-like face, had a horrid look, enough to make one fancy him really a spirit of the damned, a very devil. How his hair moved up and down on the top of his head.

He advanced upon us by starts, as it is their fashion—as I have told you in my other books—pausing to beat his fists upon his vast breast, which gave out a dull, hollow sound, like some great base-drum with a skin of ox-hide. Then, showing his enormous teeth at the same time, he made the forest ring with his short, tremendous, powerful bark, which he followed by a roar, the refrain of which is singularly like the loud muttering of thunder. The earth really shook under our feet—the noise was frightful. I have heard lions' roars, but certainly the lion's roar can not be compared with that of the gorilla.

We stood our ground for at least three long minutes—at least it seemed so to me—the guns in our hands, before the great beast was near enough for a safe shot. During this time I could not help thinking that I had heard that a man had been killed only a few days before; and, as I looked at the gorilla in front of me, I thought that if I missed the beast, I would be killed also. So I said to myself, "Be careful, friend Paul, for if you miss the fellow, he won't miss you." I realized the horror of a poor fellow when, with empty gun, he stands before his remorseless enemy, who, not with a sudden spring like the leopard, but with a slow, vindictive look, comes to put him to death.

At last he stood before us at a distance of six yards. Once more he paused, and Gambo and I raised our guns as he again began to roar and beat his chest, and just as he took another step forward, we fired, and down he tumbled, almost at our feet, upon his face—dead. But he was not the *white gorilla*.

How glad I was. I saw at once that we had killed the very animal I wanted. His height was five feet nine inches, measured to the tip of the toes. His arms spread nine feet. His chest had a circumference of sixty-two inches. His arms were of most prodigious muscular strength. His hands, those terrible, claw-like weapons, almost like a man's, having the same shaped nails, and with one blow of which he can tear out the bowels of a man and break his ribs or arms, were of immense size. I could understand how terrible a blow could be struck with such a hand, moved by such an arm, all swollen into great bunches of muscular fibres.

When I took hold of his hands, I shall not say *in* mine, for his were so large that my hands looked like those of a baby by the side of his. How cold his hands were, how callous, how thick and black the nails, as black as his face and skin. What a huge foot he possessed! Where is the giant that could show such prodigious feet?

We disemboweled the monster on the spot. Malouen and Querlaouen, who had heard our guns, joined us, and we built a camp close by. My three fellows were very fond of gorilla's meat, and they had a great treat. The brain was carefully saved by them.

In the evening Gambo told us some stories, one of which, the last one, I will relate to you. It relates to the leopard, and goes to prove that this ferocious animal has no friend.

THE LEGEND OF CONIAMBIÉ.

Coniambié was a king, who made an orambo (a trap) in which a ncheri (gazelle) was caught. After it had been caught, it cried and called for its companion; then a ngivo (another gazelle) was caught. The ngivo cried, and a wild boar came and was caught; then an antelope came, and was caught; afterward a bongo and a buffalo came, and all were caught, and all of them died in the trap. At that time Coniambié was in the mountains. A leopard was caught also, but did not die. Then came a turtle, who released the leopard from the trap. Then the leopard wanted to kill the turtle which had saved him. The leopard got hold of the turtle to kill it, but the turtle, seeing this, drew her head, legs, and tail inside her shell, but not before she had managed to get into the hollow of an old tree, with the leopard after her in the hollow, and he could not get away. The tree is called ogana, and bears a berry on which monkeys are fond of feeding. So there came to the tree at this time, for the purpose of feeding, a miengai, or white-mustached monkey; a ndova, the white-nosed monkey; a nkago, the red-headed monkey; an oganagana, a blackish monkey; a mondi, which has very long black hair; a nchegai and a pondi, who all came to eat the berries. When the leopard heard the noise of the monkeys, he shouted, "Monkeys, come and release me!" Then they came and helped the leopard out of the hole. But the leopard, instead of being grateful, fought with the monkeys, and ate the nkago and the ndova. Then the monkey called a mpondi said, "*Mai! mai!* That is so; that is so! You leopards are noted rogues. The leopard and the goat do not live together at the same place. We came to help you, and, as soon as you were helped, you began to kill us. *Mai! mai!* you are a rogue."

Moral.

The reason why the leopard wanders solitary and alone is on account of his roguery; he is not to be trusted. There are men who can not be trusted any more than the leopard.

We shouted with one voice, "That is so; there are men who can not be any more trusted than the leopard, for they are so treacherous and deceitful."

Then we canvassed the bad qualities of the leopard, and concluded that he had not a single friend in the forest.

After this story was concluded we gave another look to our fires, and then went to sleep. This was the way, Young Folks, we spent many of our evenings when we were not too tired traveling in the great forest.

CHAPTER VII.

RETURN TO THE OVENGA RIVER.—THE MONKEYS AND THEIR FRIENDS THE BIRDS.—THEY LIVE TOGETHER.—WATCH BY MOONLIGHT FOR GAME.—KILL AN OSHENGUI.

AFTER wandering through the forest for many days, we reached once more the banks of the River Rembo Ovenga, the waters of which had fallen twelve or fifteen feet, for we are in the dry season. The numerous aquatic birds and waders which come with the dry weather give the river a lively, pleasant appearance. The white sand which lines many parts of the shore is beautiful. The mornings are cool, and sometimes foggy. The dark green of the well-wooded banks had something grand about it. I, poor and lonely traveler, had a charming scene before me. The stream is still yellow, but far less so than in the rainy season. Then the rains were driving down a turbulent tide laden with mud washed down from the mountains and valleys; now the waters roll on placidly, as though all was peace and civilization on their borders.

New birds had come. The otters were plentiful, and fed on the fish that were thick in the stream.

In that great jungle beasts had been scarce for some time, and we had a hard time to get food.

But what a glorious time we had by ourselves in that forest! Oh how I enjoyed rambling in that jungle, though toiling hard, and often hungry and sick! How glad I always was when I returned to the banks of the Rembo Ovenga! I loved that river, for I knew that its waters, as they glided down, would disappear in that very ocean whose waves bathed the shores of both the Old and the New World. At times, when seated on its banks, I could not help it, I would think of friends absent, but dear to me. I remembered those I loved—I remembered the boys and girls who were slowly but surely growing men and women, but who were still young folks in my memory, though years were flying fast. The lad of the jungle had become a man also; his mustache had made its appearance, and had grown a good deal; his face had become older—probably he found it so when perchance he gazed in the looking-glass he carried with him. Disease, anxiety, sleepless nights, and traveling under the burning sun had begun to do their work; but, in despite of all, my heart was still young, and I loved more than ever those friends I had left behind.

I had come back to Obindji to see if I could get some plantains or smoked cassada, and then intended to return to the woods in search of new animals and new insects. King Obindji welcomed me, and was delighted to see Malaouen, Querlaouen, and Gambo once more, and his wives got food ready for us. Then we started again for the forest. I took with me lots of small shot of different sizes for birds, and once more we would get lost in the jungle, but from time to time we would come back to the uninhabited banks of the wild Ovenga to look at our river.

One day, wandering in the forest, I spied a queer-looking bird I had not seen before, and I immediately got ready to chase it. This bird was called by the natives the monkey-bird (*Buceros albocrystatus*).

As I was looking at that queer bird I spied a monkey, two monkeys, three monkeys, four, five, six, ten monkeys. These monkeys looked very small, and were called oshengui by the natives. Then I saw more of the queer birds,

WATCHING BIRDS AND MONKEYS.

and lo! I perceived they were all playing with these little monkeys—yes, playing with these oshenguis.

Strange indeed they looked, with their long-feathered tail, queer-looking body, and strange big beak. They followed those little monkeys as they leaped from branch

C 2

to branch; sometimes I thought they would rest on the backs of the monkeys, but no, they would perch close to them, and then the monkey and the bird would look at each other. I never heard a note from the birds—they were as silent as the trees themselves. The oshengui would look at them and utter a kind of kee, kee, kee, and then they would move on, and the birds would follow.

Day after day I would meet those birds, and then I would look for the monkeys, and was sure to see them. No wonder they are called the monkey-bird. But then I never saw them follow any monkeys but the oshengui. I wondered why they followed them; I could not imagine the reason. I never saw them resting on the birds, but I noticed that these birds were fond of the fruits and berries the oshneguis feed upon. Then the question arose, Did the birds follow the monkeys, or the monkeys the birds? I came to the conclusion that the birds followed the monkeys, whom they could hear telling them, as it were, where they could get food without searching for it.

I tried to discover where these birds made their nests, but never found one in the country of the Rembo.

Now let us come to their companions, the monkeys. How small are these oshenguis! They are the smallest monkeys of that part of Africa. Their color was of a yellowish tinge; they had long, but not prehensile tails, for the monkeys with prehensile tails are found in America. It is a frolicsome and innocent little animal. Strange to say, the common people, who eat all kinds of monkeys, would not eat that one—why, I could not tell. His cry is very plaintive and sad, and is not heard far off, like the cry of other monkeys. As sure as you live, when you meet them hopping about the branches overhead, you may say that water is not far off. They always sleep on trees whose branches overhang a water-course. They all sleep on the same tree. How queer they look, with their tails hanging down! To see the mother carrying her young, and the young clinging to the mother, is a sight worth seeing, for these baby monkeys do not look bigger than rats, and, when quite young, not much bigger than large mice. Strange to say, though very young monkeys can not walk, from the very day they are born they seem to be able to cling with their hands to the breast of their mother; for young monkeys must help themselves, or they would drop to the ground.

So we may say that the oshengui and the monkey-bird are almost inseparable friends, and we must let them wander in the great jungle in search of their food while we look for other birds and animals.

There were also in the forest several varieties of tiger-cat, the name of which is very similar to that of the little monkeys, the oshengui, I have just spoken to you about.

There are several species of these cats, but I am going to speak to you of the *Genetta Fieldiana*. You will say, "What a queer name!" Not at all. I have told you that I often remembered him in Africa, and I named this animal after my friend, Mr. Cyrus W. Field. I described this animal in the proceedings of the Boston Natural History Society.

These oshenguis are perfect little plagues. They are very sly; they never sleep at night; they are then wandering in search of prey—of something to kill. They see better at night than in broad daylight. During the day they hide in some hollow tree, or in the midst of a cluster of thick, dead branches, which are so close together that you can not see what is inside. They will crawl in there and remain till night comes. The darker the night, the bolder their deeds; for on a dark night they will come into the villages, knowing that every body is generally asleep between two or three o'clock in the morning, manage to get into some poultry-house—I do not know how—and then pounce upon the poor chickens and strangle them. They will destroy the whole lot of them, suck their blood, and if they can, they will drag one away. If you have a parrot they will try to get at it. Sometimes they will climb trees and get their prey among the birds. The green wild pigeons, the partridges, the wild ducks and cranes, sleeping on the banks of rivers, are good food for them, for they are very fond of the feathered tribe.

One morning, on the banks of a creek not far from our camp, I saw the footprints of an oshengui on the sands. It had been there, I could see, the night before.

I had two or three chickens, which I kept carefully. I wanted to see if I could not get a few eggs, for I had not for a long time tasted any, and I wondered if the oshengui would come and eat my chickens. Poor chickens! they have to look sharp in that country, for they have many enemies among the snakes and the species of wild-cats of the forest, besides the hawks.

The moon was declining, and rose about one o'clock in the morning, and shone just bright enough to enable me to see. So, towards one o'clock, I took one of my chickens and tied it to a stick on the bank of the little creek near our camp, and hid myself, not far off, on the edge of the forest. I took with me two guns, one loaded with bullets in case I should meet larger game I did not bargain for, and the other loaded with shot, which I intended for the oshengui, if it came.

The light from the moon was dim, as I have said, but just enough for me to see. I hoped that the oshengui would come from the direction opposite to where I was. The poor fowl began to cackle, frightened at being in a strange place, and no doubt having an instinctive knowledge of insecurity. It cackled and cackled from time to time, and then would try to go to sleep, but could not; it seemed to comprehend impending danger.

At last I saw something coming along the shore whose eyes were like two bright charcoal fires. It seemed so close to the ground that, if it had not been for the two fiery eyes, I should have thought it was a big snake. The legs were so short and so bent that the body touched the ground. I raised my gun very carefully, and waited. At last I could see the long muzzle of the oshengui. How sly the animal was! He came on like a thief, and so carefully looking right and left as he advanced, but never losing sight of the fowl. The nearer he came, the flatter his body lay on the ground, until it arrived near the fowl; then there was a pause; then a sudden spring upon the fowl—there was just one cry; the fowl was dead. Having aimed carefully, I pulled the trigger—bang! and down rolled the oshengui on his back, with the fowl in his jaws. A tremendous shout rose from our camp. Gambo, Querlaouen, and Malaouen came rushing toward me, and they all cried, "You will kill no more of our fowls now, Oshengui!" With my prize hung above my head, I went to sleep, and the next day we made preparations to go up the river.

CHAPTER VIII.

WE ARE IN A CANOE.—OUTFIT FOR HUNTING.—SEE A BEAUTIFUL ANTELOPE. — KILL IT. — IT IS A NEW SPECIES. — RIVER AND FOREST SWALLOWS.

WE are now ascending the River Rembo Ovenga. We are in a little canoe, that can be easily hidden in the jungle, and as we ascend the river we meet strange sights, and I can assure you we enjoy our journey. It is true that it is hot, but we can not help it. In the bow of the canoe is a little stick, to which is attached a nice little flag showing the Stars and Stripes. Querlaouen is at the stern, and using his paddle as a rudder; Malaouen is at the head, where he keeps a sharp look-out for wild beasts. I need not say that his gun is close at hand.

Gambo and I have our paddles, and we dip them gently—so gently that, if you had been on the banks of the river at night, you could not have heard us. Near the prow is a smooth-bore gun, loaded with shot, in case we should see some big crane or wild ducks. By my side lies a double-barreled breech-loader, loaded with very large steel-pointed bullets, in case of need, for elephants, crocodiles, leopards, wild buffaloes, and gorillas; or, should we be attacked by the savages inhabiting the country, they were to be used against them. By the side of that gun was a heavy war-axe. Malaouen had his gun by him; Gambo likewise. Our formidable double-barreled breech-loader, with steel-pointed bullets, would smash, I was sure, an elephant's ribs, if the opportunity occurred. We had an extra gun, in case one should get out of order. We had also two cutlasses. We thought we would dispense with a cooking-pot, for all our food was to be roasted on charcoal — that is to say, if we were able to kill any game. In a little box made of tin I had matches, a few flints, and a fire-steel, which were to be used in case the matches should become worthless.

I had also a lancet, a little bottle of ammonia to be used in the event of either of us being bitten by a scorpion or some venomous serpent, some medicine, and a bottle of quinine.

For food we had a few plantains and dried cassada. Then we expected to find berries, nuts, and fruits, and wild honey. Of course our imagination ran wild. The idea of Gambo was that the forest would be full of wild game; antelopes were to be plentiful, and also wild boars.

Our outfit was of the light order. Gambo, Malaouen, and Querlaouen wore next to nothing, and they had no change of clothes but a wild-cat skin. They could take it easy in the matter of clothing—shirts, neck-ties, pantaloons, waistcoats, and coats were superfluities which they can dispense with.

My outfit was composed of the clothes I wore, and in my hunting-bag I had an extra pair of thick shoes, in case those I wore should give out, and a second pair of pantaloons.

Each of us had a flask full of powder, with a goodly number of bullets, and some small shot.

At last we came to the spot where we wanted to land,

and then hauled our canoe into the jungle, hiding it where we thought no one could see it. Afterward we advanced a little into the forest, and then made our camp for the night. As usual, we made large, blazing fires, and, after they had been fairly started, we laid down on the green branches of the trees we had cut, and before I knew it my men were fast asleep. The deep snore of Gambo told me that he was unconscious of what was going on around; he was soon followed by Querlaouen and Malaouen, and they snorted a trio which would have well frightened any wild beast which might come lurking round us. Each of these men held their guns closely in their arms.

I rose and looked at these three brave and daring savages, who now slumbered perfectly unconscious and helpless. I looked at them with a feeling of love, and thought that soon, like themselves, I would fall asleep, and be as unconscious of all that was round me. I thought of the wild country I was in, of the wild beasts by which I was surrounded, and I began to feel so little and so weak, I seated myself and prayed to the great God, he who had created the white man, and the black man, and all species of men, and the wild beasts of the forest, to keep me as he had done before.

Continuing our wanderings in the forest, the next morning I came alone to a beautiful little stream, and just as I was in the act of stooping to drink some of its water, which was as clear as crystal, I suddenly heard a slight noise not far off, which I believed must be made by antelopes or gazelles. Looking carefully at my gun, I made for that part of the forest from whence came the sounds, trying to be as nimble and as noiseless as I could. I had not proceeded far when my eyes opened wide open, and I became terribly excited, for I saw an animal I had never seen before—an antelope. It was the most lovely and beautiful creature of the forest I had ever seen. I stopped. It seemed to me that I had not eyes big enough to admire it. Oh, I thought, it is too beautiful to be fired at and killed. How brilliant was his colors! The body was of a bright yellow, as bright as an orange; then from its back came fourteen beautiful stripes, as white as snow; a chestnut patch between the horns and the eyes, below which was a white crescent, having in the middle a dark brown stripe. That beautiful creature was quietly resting on the trunk of a dead tree, while beyond, among the trees, were several others which I could not see so well.

I was so excited I could not breathe, for of all the lovely beasts I had seen in the forest, this one was the most lovely; none could have compared with it in beauty. The skin of the leopard was nothing to it.

I raised my gun almost in sorrow, but I felt that I must kill the beast, in order to bring its skin home; for I knew it was an animal that had never been seen before.

Just as I raised my gun, the beautiful creature rose up from the tree on which it had slept, as if to show me its beautiful form, and how graceful were its motions, before the fatal shot should put an end to its life. I wish you could have seen this antelope when alive, surrounded by the green of the forest, which contrasted singularly with its bright color, and made the animal appear as if it had come from an enchanted land, where the sun had given to its hair and skin its own golden color, as it sometimes

SHOOTING THE NEW ANTELOPE.

gives it to the clouds when it is on the point of disappearing.

I put my finger on the trigger and fired; down came that beautiful creature from the tree, falling on its back, showing a stomach as white as milk. The others decamped without my being able to fire at them, on account of the fallen tree.

As I came near to look at my great prize, I felt that I would like to put my arm round the nice neck of the animal, whose short groans betokened it was in the agonies of death, for I felt so sorry, and I wished I could see it alive again. Then the blood poured from its mouth, and stained the ground on which it lay gasping for breath, which it could not get. After a few struggles all became silent; the poor antelope was dead, killed by the ruthless hand of man.

I looked at it and looked at it, for I could not tire looking at such a beautiful beast.

The men came, and we cut a heavy branch of a tree, to which we fastened it, and brought the poor dead antelope to the camp. When I brought the stuffed animal to a village, the people at once shouted with transports of the wildest astonishment, "Bongo! bongo!" for such was the native name given to this antelope.

I need not say how careful I was in preparing its skin, which to me was precious, and I brought the stuffed specimen back to New York in the year 1859, and in 1860 it could have been seen among the large collection I had brought here.*

The collection has left the country.

* A description of it can be seen in the report of the Boston Natural History Society for 1860.

Since the day I had killed the bongo we had built another camp near another beautiful stream—the forest was full of them—and not far from two or three abandoned plantations. Often I would go all alone and watch the birds. I loved especially to look at the swallows One which I discovered was a beautiful species. It is all black, but with a bluish tinge. When the weather was clear, and there was no prospect of an approaching storm, they flew high in the air; but if the weather was threatening, they would almost touch the bushes. When they fly high in the air, the insects on which they feed, I suppose, are there; but when a storm is coming the insects no doubt know it, and come down to seek refuge from the rain under the leaves or blades of grass. These are the reasons by which I account for the swallows flying high in fine weather, and low when a storm is coming.

How quickly these little black swallows did fly! None of them had ever seen our northern clime. They were birds of the equatorial regions of Africa. The woods are their home, and the open spots where plantations or villages are built, and where the rivers flow, are the places where they love to fly in search of their food.

There was another beautiful swallow, a river swallow, black in color, with a solitary white spot, which looked like silver, on its throat. What a beautiful little bird it is! Its days were spent flying over the river. It would take a flight, and then rest on the branches or stumps of some dead trees which were imbedded in the stream, but the branches of which were just above the water.

I could not help feeling sorry when killing these little birds, and, after I thought I had killed enough of them to enrich the museums, nothing would have tempted me to kill another.

This lovely and dear little swallow has never seen the countries where the polar star is visible; the silence of the forest is its delight, and its pleasure is to skim over the waters of rivers which come from unexplored and unpenetrated mountains, where the name of the white man has never been heard.

How I loved to look at these little birds, for I do love swallows!

Little wanderers they are. At home they are the heralds of spring. If they could speak, how many touching stories they would have to tell us of their wonderful escapes, and of their trials and dangers; what hardships they have to encounter when they migrate and travel over distant lands, when they cross over seas and over mountains; how many of them fall bravely before reaching the land they want to reach; what stormy and tempestuous weather they often meet in their journey, and how happy they must feel when they have come to the land of their migration.

CHAPTER IX.

WE HEAR THE CRY OF A YOUNG GORILLA.—START TO CAPTURE HIM.—FIGHT WITH "HIS FATHER."—WE KILL HIM.—KILL THE MOTHER.—CAPTURE OF THE BABY.—STRANGE CAMP SCENE.

ONE very fine morning, just at the dawn of day, when the dew-drops were falling from leaf to leaf, and could hardly reach the ground; just as the birds were beginning to sing, the insects to hum, the bee to buzz, the butterflies to awake, I suddenly heard the cry of a young gorilla for his mother. Malaouen and Querlaouen were with me. They heard the cry as well as I did, and immediately gave a kind of *chuck* for me to remain still. We listened attentively to ascertain the exact spot in the forest whence the noise proceeded. Another cry from the young gorilla told us the precise direction, and we made for the place.

The jungle was so thick that we had to be most careful in order to avoid arousing the suspicions of the gorilla. Happily, we came to a little rivulet which seemed to flow from the direction in which we had heard the noise. So we waded into it and followed its course instead of a path. The water at times reached as high as our knees; it was cool and limpid, and the bed of the stream was gravelly.

The noise made by the young gorilla had for some

time ceased, and we wondered if he had gone. When, lo! I heard a heavy chuckle—it was the mother! We were not far off. We left the stream, passing through the jungle most carefully. At last we lay flat on our bellies, looking more like snakes than human beings. I had that morning painted my face and hands black, so I appeared of the same color as my men. We crawled to a spot where we remained quite still, for we could then hear the noise the mother gorilla made in taking the berries from the lower branches of the trees, or in tearing down some wild kind of cane. We were watching and peering through the jungle—my eyes were almost sore from the exertion.

By-and-by we heard a noise in our rear. It was the male gorilla! What a terrific roar he gave as he saw us close by, and watching his wife. The whole forest resounded with it. Goodness gracious! I thought we ought to have been more careful. We ought to have considered that perhaps the male gorilla was with his wife. But in less time than I take to write it we were facing the gorilla, who advanced toward us, his face convulsed with rage. Just as he was close upon us we fired, and he fell forward on his face, uttering a most frightful groan. After a few movements and twitchings of the limbs, he was silent, for he was dead.

In the mean time the mother and her young had gone off, leaving the "big fellow" to fight their battles.

It was a good thing that the big gorilla came first, for he might have come after we had fired, and while we were trying to catch "his child," and then pounced upon us.

"The female gorilla and her young have gone; but

first," said Malaouen, "let us hide ourselves close by and wait; perhaps she will come back; let us see if we can not find them." We hid ourselves on the lower branches of a tree, not far from the dead body of the big gorilla. We waited and waited—not a sound—nothing to show that the female gorilla was coming back to see if her mate was there.

Beginning to feel somewhat tired of waiting, I said, "Boys, let us see if we can find the gorilla. You know, as well as I do, that female gorilla are timid—indeed, that most of them are great cowards. The 'men' gorilla fight, but the 'women' gorilla do not."

"That is so," replied Malaouen. "Querlaouen, let us go after the female and try to capture her."

So we descended the tree upon which we had hidden ourselves. We left the big gorilla dead on the ground, bidding him good-by, and telling him that we were coming again; Malaouen adding in a queer way, "Kombo" (that is the name they give to a male gorilla), "who told you to come and fight us? If you had not come, perhaps at this time you might have been by the side of your wife and child, instead of being asleep for all time to come. The forest is not going to hear your 'talk' any more, and you are not going to frighten any body." So we left the big fellow dead on the ground, and went immediately in search of the female gorilla and her young.

In order not to lose our dead gorilla, as we advanced in the jungle, we broke, here and there, young branches of the trees, and from time to time collected leaves in our hands, which we dropped on the ground, and then, on our return, we would look after the boughs of the trees we had broken, and the leaves we had scattered, and thus find our way back to the gorilla.

We traveled on through the jungle for a long time, and no gorilla. At last we were startled. We heard a roar. It was the female calling for her mate. It was the female that had escaped from us in the morning. She was calling for the "old man," who would not hear her any more, for, as you know, he was dead. She called and called, but there was no answer for her.

Carefully we went through the jungle, stepping gently on the dead leaves of the trees till we came near the female gorilla, which we saw just behind an old tree that had fallen on the ground. There she was, looking at her babe, giving now and then a kind of chuckle, her old, wrinkled black face looking so ugly. Her gray eyes followed the young gorilla as he would move round; then she would pick a berry, giving another kind of chuckle for the baby to come and get it. After eating it he would climb on his mother, and she would pass her thick black hand over the little body. Then he came down and seated himself between her legs, and gazed at her, his little black face looking so queer. Then he moved off again, but only to return once more. As I was very intently watching, my gun slipped from the tree along which it rested, and fell on the ground. The gorilla heard it, gave a shriek, and, followed by her babe, was starting to run. The gun of Querlaouen was too quick for her. Bang! The poor mother fell in her gore, but the little fellow disappeared in the woods.

We leaped over the tree, and did not even take a look at the poor dead gorilla, but rushed in pursuit of the young fellow, who was the prize we wanted the most.

D

At last we saw him; a stream had stopped his flight. He could not get any farther, and was looking toward the other side. But he soon spied us, and took to a young sapling, and when he had reached the top he looked at us with glaring eyes, and—would you believe it?—howled again and again at us!

There was no way to get at him, so Malaouen took his axe, and down came the tree, with the gorilla on it, howling and shrieking. At the same instant Querlaouen threw over his head a little net we carried with us for the purpose of capturing gorillas, and so we caught him.

We hollaed and shouted also, so our shouts, mixed with the howls and shrieks of the gorilla, made a charming concert in the jungle. After giving vent to our joyous feelings by shouts, and had sobered down again, I wish you could have seen that gorilla kicking under its net. The question was how to take the fellow from under the net and get it home. I cried, "Give me the axe; I see a branch close by which will make a splendid forked stick." The words were hardly uttered before the axe was in my hands, and in the wink of an eye I had hold of a stick about five feet long, with a pronged fork. Malaouen had in the mean time cut a little stick to tie across it, and collected some creepers to be used as cords.

I wish you could have heard his howls as Querlaouen seized the little villain by the back of his head, while I put the forked stick on his neck, holding it fast to the ground while Malaouen was tying the little stick, now and then taking his hands off for fear of a bite, the little rascal kicked up such a row. Querlaouen, who had become free to act after I got the forked stick firm over his neck, had all he could do to hold the legs of the little fellow on the ground, who kicked up, hollaed, and shrieked; his muscles worked, and he tried to catch hold of us with his hands, but the forked stick was too much for him, and then we succeeded in tying his hands behind his back.

I was sorry to hurt his poor neck, but the first thing the little rascal attempted as soon as I raised the stick from the ground was to start at us. But he could not even turn his head round. He had to walk off a prisoner, and his shouts and shrieks were of no avail. His father and mother had been killed, and he had no one to defend him from his enemies.

How proud we felt of our prize! We returned by the way we had come, being guided by the broken boughs of young trees and the leaves we had thrown on the ground. As soon as we came to the female gorilla, and the little fellow saw his mother, he tried to rush toward her. I dropped the forked stick and let him go. He at once jumped on his mother, and began sucking her breasts, and then looked in her face, and appeared to feel quite sorrowful. When he saw she was dead, he gave a howl at us, as if to say, "You fellows have killed my mother!"

It was utterly impossible for us to carry to our camp all our spoil, so we concluded to hang her to a branch of a tree, and come for her the next morning, which we did.

Then we continued our march, and toward sunset came to the large male we had killed in the morning. We were so tired that we did not wish to do any thing with the big gorilla that night. I felt I was too tired to take his skin off. The little fellow did not seem to care for his father; he looked at him well, and gave only a single plaintive cry. I could not help thinking of the poor old fellow. How many times he had slept at the foot of some big tree, and kept watch over his wife and baby! Now he was dead, nothing but his huge body and his tremendous face showed the giant strength he once possessed; now a little insect was stronger than he was.

What had he died for? He had died bravely defending his wife and baby from an enemy whom he knew had come to do them harm. He was right. May I and every man of us always have the same motive that big gorilla had!

I could not help feeling sorry. Here lay dead before me a wonderful beast, one of the most strange creatures of the forest God has created. His mate lay dead in another part of the forest, and their offspring was my prisoner.

How strange his huge shadow looked as he hung by the neck to the limb of a tree near our camp, and how small our bodies looked by the side of his!

That night I could not sleep. That big gorilla was always before my eyes. He seemed to grin at me; his long, powerful arm, his huge hands, appeared as if they were moving and trying to seize me. I could see his big black nails ready to go into my flesh; his mouth seemed ready to open and give one of those terrific roars which shake the whole forest. And then I would see his enormous canines come out from his sharp-cut lips, and how red his mouth was inside. There were his deep sunken eyes, wide open, looking at me, and, though dead, he had a scowl of defiance and intense ferocity on his face. It so happened that his face was turned toward the bed of leaves on which I lay, and he was hung not far from me.

The young gorilla during the whole night moaned for his mother. He would look at the fires before him, then at us, and then give a howl, as if he was saying, "What have I before me?" I decidedly frightened him more than Malaouen and Querlaouen could, for, in despite of the noise the young gorilla made, and of the shadow of the big gorilla, they had fallen sound asleep. But now and then they would awake, look at the fires, put on more wood to make a blaze, would perhaps smoke a pipe, and then go to sleep again.

Toward four o'clock in the morning Querlaouen arose, took from his bag a little idol, and put it on the ground, muttering words I could not hear, all the time thinking I was sound asleep. Then he took a piece of chalk of the Alumbi, and rubbed it on his forehead between his two eyes; then he rubbed it in the hollow of his chest, and along both his arms; then he chewed a piece of a certain soft cane, which he spat on the idol; and then he talked to it. Now and then he muttered my name. At last I understood that the ignorant but good fellow was begging his idol to take care of me.

Then, with his sharp-pointed knife, he cut his two hands slightly in many places, and took the blood that fell and rubbed his body with it, also the idol, and then laid down once more by the fires and took another sleep.

Gambo had left us to go after wild honey, but not before making us a solemn promise not to hunt gorilla, for I was afraid that some accident might happen to him. The next morning when he returned to our camp, and saw our big gorilla hanging to the tree, and heard that the mother of the young gorilla had been killed also, he

QUERLAOUEN AND HIS IDOL.

cried, "Why did I go after wild honey instead of remaining with you!" But he quietly seated himself, and after a while wanted a piece of gorilla for his breakfast, for we had to skin the beast, as I wanted his hide and skeleton.

The next evening I saw the shelter of a nshiego-mbouvé (*Troglodytes calvus*). I crept within shot of the shelter, lay down flat in the jungle—I am sure a snake or leopard could not have lain more quiet—and there I waited. My men had covered themselves with dry leaves and brush, scarce daring to breathe, lest the approaching animal should hear us.

From the calls there were evidently two. It was getting dark in the forest, and I began to feel afraid that the animals had smelt us, when I saw a nshiego-mbouvé approach the tree where the shelter was. It ascended by a hand-over-hand movement, and with great rapidity. Then it crept carefully under the shelter, seated itself in the crotch made by a projecting bough, its feet and haunches resting on this bough, then put one arm round the trunk of the tree for security. Thus they rest all night, and this posture accounts for some singular abrasions of the hair on the side of this variety of chimpanzee, which could be seen on the specimens I brought home.

No sooner was it seated than it began again to utter its call. It was a male, and was calling for its female. It was answered, when an unlucky motion of one of my men made a noise, and roused the suspicions of the ape in the tree. It looked round. It began preparations to descend and clear out. I fired, and it fell to the ground dead, with a tremendous crash.

These nshiego-mbouvé are very shy, and far more difficult to approach than gorillas. How queer they look with their bald heads! The black skin on the top of the head is quite shiny. They must attain great age, and I have often wondered how long the gorilla, chimpanzee, kooloo-kamba, and nshiego-mbouvé live. I should not be surprised if they sometimes live to be a hundred years old.

All the varieties of chimpanzees often inhabit the same woods as the gorilla, and they seem to live in harmony with each other. There is food enough for them all; besides, nuts and fruits are very plentiful. When they get old they feed on leaves, for a time comes when their teeth are quite decayed. In one very old nshiego-mbouvé I killed, nearly all of his teeth had dropped out, and he had but four or five left.

CHAPTER X.

JACK WILL HAVE HIS OWN WAY.—HE SEIZES MY LEG.—
HE TEARS MY PANTALOONS.—HE GROWLS AT ME.—HE
REFUSES COOKED FOOD.—JACK MAKES HIS BED.—JACK
SLEEPS WITH ONE EYE OPEN.—JACK IS INTRACTABLE.

Now let us follow that young gorilla, whom I called Jack.

Jack, to begin with, was the most untractable little beast one possibly could get hold of. Jack was a little villain, a little rogue, very treacherous, and quite untamable. The kinder I was, the worse he seemed to be. We took him with us in the forest till we returned to our village, and then many of the women disappeared.

Jack was smart in his wickedness, and was quite as treacherous as any of the gorillas I had met before. He would not eat any cooked food, and every day I had to send into the forest for berries and nuts. I wish you could have seen his eyes glisten, you would have noticed how treacherous and gloomy they were. Jack was cunning; he would look at me right straight in the face, and when he did that I learned that he meant mischief, and, if close at hand, meant an attack upon me.

Of course, once in the camp, the forked stick had been taken away, and a little chain tied round the neck of Jack; the chain was about six feet long. Then I had a long pole fastened in the ground, and the chain was tied to an iron ring which had been used as a bracelet on the upper arm of a native, by which means he could turn all round without entangling the chain.

One day I had come to offer Jack some tondo (berries) which friend Malaouen had just collected for him (I wanted always to feed Jack myself, to see if I could tame him), and I approached the little fellow to within the distance which I thought the utmost length of his chain would allow him to go. He looked at me straight in the face, and I waited for him to extend his arm to get the nice tondo I was offering him, when, quick as lightning, he threw his body on the ground on one arm and

CAUGHT BY JACK.

one leg, the chain drawn to its full length, and then, before I knew it, he seized my leg, and with his big toe got hold and fast of my *inexpressibles*, which were rather old, and a portion of them was soon in his possession.

I thought in my fright that a piece of my leg had also been taken away, which I am glad to say was not the case. Still holding the piece of my pantaloons, he retreated to his pole, then gave a howl and started at me again. This time I knew better—I was off. He held the piece of my pantaloons for a long time, it having passed from his big toe into his hand.

Jack looked at times almost cross-eyed, and was as ugly a fellow as any one could wish to see. He was not so strong as friend Joe, the account of which you have read in "Stories of the Gorilla Country," but he was a pretty strong chap, and I should not have liked to be shut up in a room alone with him. Several times I had narrow escapes of a grip from his strong big toe.

When evening came, Jack would collect the dry leaves I had given him, and would go to sleep upon them, and sometimes he did look almost like a child.

How strange that I never saw twin gorillas! The mother gorilla has only one baby gorilla at a time. My men and I have captured a good many of their young ones during the time I lived in the great forest of Equatorial Africa, but I never succeeded in taming one. Some were more fierce or stubborn than others, but all refused food that was cooked; the berries, nuts, and fruits must come from the forest. Though these little brutes were diminutive, and the merest babies in age, they were astonishingly strong, and, as you have yourselves seen in the different accounts I have given you, by no means good tempered. When any thing displeased them they would roar, and bellow, and look wickedly from out their cunning little eyes, and strike the ground with their feet.

Jack was not so ugly-looking a fellow as friend Joe,

neither was he as strong. Like all the gorillas, his face and his skin were entirely black. His little eyes, deep and sunken, seemed to be gray; his nose was more prominent than in the chimpanzee, for gorillas have noses, and consequently he comes nearer in appearance than the chimpanzee to the African negro. He had, as we have, eyelashes, and the upper ones were the longest. His mouth was large, and the lips sharply cut. The gorilla has no lips like we have; the dark pigment covers them, and when his mouth is shut no red is seen outside. The ears are small in comparison with the face, and they are smaller than the ears of man. Their ears are much smaller than those of the chimpanzee, and look very much like the ears of man; the chin is short and receding.

The face is very wrinkled; the head is covered with hair much shorter than that on the body, and in the male gorilla the top of the head has a reddish crown of hair.

You see how much the arm of the gorilla is like the arm of man—how short his legs are. The leg is about the same size from the knee to the ankle, the short thigh decreasing slightly. The leg of the gorilla has not the graceful curve found in man, it having no calf.

I want you to examine the hands and feet of a young gorilla. You will be struck at once how short the hand is, and how much it looks like that of a man. The fingers are short, but how thick they are! the nails are very much like ours, and project slightly over the tips of the fingers. See how short the thumb is—how much shorter than the thumb of man; it is hardly half as thick as the forefinger. The thumb is of very little use to a gorilla. The palm of the hand is hard, naked, and callous; the back is hairy to the knuckles, and the short hair grows on the fingers, as in man.

GORILLA SLEEPING.

The leg of the gorilla is very short. Look at his foot. Instead of a big toe he has a thumb, and you see, by the wrinkles and transverse indents, that the foot is used as a hand. The third toe is a little longer than the second, and the others follow in the same proportion; and, if you look at your own feet, you will see that the toes of the gorilla and those of man keep the same gradation of length, the middle one being the longest.

Look at the representation of a young gorilla as he sleeps. He certainly looks almost like a baby; but do not believe that he is so fast asleep that you need make a great deal of noise to awake him. No; these little fellows seem to go "to bed" with one eye open, and at the least noise you see their gray eye twinkle, and immediately they sit up, and look round to discover what is the matter, and at once are ready for a fight. As they awake they generally give a howl of defiance.

CHAPTER XI.

START AFTER LAND-CRABS.—VILLAGE OF THE CRABS.—EACH CRAB KNOWS HIS HOUSE.—GREAT FLIGHT OF CRABS.—THEY BITE HARD.—FEAST ON THE SLAIN.—A HERD OF HIPPOPOTAMI.

We have come down to the river. We are off in our canoes to hunt for ogombon (land-crabs), each one of us being provided with a basket and a short cutlass, and are paddling for some spot not far from the banks of the river where the land-crabs are found in abundance. There are several canoes full of women, for catching crabs is the special business of the women, as hunting is the special work of the men.

The land-crabs burrow in the ground. Their holes are found in very large numbers in some parts of the country. The burrows form the subterranean homes of the crabs, into which they retire when alarmed—and the slightest noise does that. They remain in their burrows until hunger drives them out in search of food, or when they fancy danger is averted.

We landed at last on a swampy bottom, the soil of which was very black. I immediately saw an innumerable quantity of crabs running in all directions—making for their burrows—alarmed at our approach and the sound of footsteps; and as they ran they displayed the two large claws with which they were ready to bite any one bold enough to seize them. The ground was covered with an incredible number of burrows.

These land-crabs are curious creatures. They are found in various parts of the world, and Equatorial Africa has a fair share of them, in goodly variety. The natives have any number of wonderful tales to tell about the ogombons.

There was a wild shout of joy among the people at having come to the right spot. The baskets were immediately opened, the short heavy sticks and cutlasses were got in readiness, and we scattered all over the thickly-wooded island, for it was an island where only mangrove grew. Not far from the island I could see huge hippopotami playing in the river, but we had taken it into our heads to come down the river and make a great haul of these crustaceæ.

There was, as I have said, a general skedaddle of crabs, for at the least noise they ran away, having a counterpart in the women, who ran to and fro with great shouts, which were soon taken up by the men, in their wild excitement after land-crabs.

These crabs were of tremendous size, and were the real ogombons, the largest species found in the country, and the only ones the natives will eat. They were gray, almost of the color of the mud on which they walk. They were armed with tremendous claws, which warned us to be very careful in handling them, or we should get a good bite.

This island was celebrated as the home of the ogombons, and the whole of that part on which we landed was entirely covered with their burrows, which were in many places so thick and so close together as to communicate with each other. In these retreats the crabs remain in darkness. They never venture far from home. How Master Land-Crab knows his own habitation from those of his neighbor I can not tell, but now and then he would make a mistake and go into "somebody else's house," thus getting into the wrong box.

At this time of the year the land-crabs were fat, but the shells were somewhat hard, but not so hard as later in the season, when the crab is left to himself, not being so good to eat. Hence, in the season, land-crab parties start from every village for the spots where they are to be found.

When the crabs are ready to cast off their shells, they shut themselves up in their burrow, which they have stocked with leaves, closing the entrance with mud, and they remain there until their new armor is on. After quitting its old armor a crab is very soft, but in course of time the new shell becomes hard, even harder than the preceding one. I was never able to ascertain the age a land-crab could attain.

So we were racing in every direction after the land-crabs, which fled with the utmost speed for their burrows. Now and then one would be caught. We had to be very light of foot when approaching them, for at the least noise they would go and hide in their dark abodes.

Of the two large claws, one was a tremendous thing, and it was amusing to watch the crabs walking leisurely round their holes, as if there was no foe in their neighborhood, but yet holding up one of the large claws as if they were ready for any thing that might come along. This claw nodded backward and forward in a very comical manner.

I approached one very big fellow without his having perceived me, and, before he was aware, I laid my stick heavily on his back, and then seized him with my hand, to place him in the basket which hung at my side. I roared out with pain, for he had got hold of one of my fingers with its large claw, and shook it as if he would have torn it off. With my other hand I quickly seized

CATCHING THE OGOMBONS.

the crab and twisted the claws from the body, which I thought would release me; but lo! although the body lay on the ground, the rascally claws gripped harder than ever. Oh! oh! oh!!! I shouted—which cries brought two or three of the women to my assistance. The muscles of the claws had retained their contractile power after they were separated from the body.

In the mean time the rascal had retired into his burrow, no doubt in a good deal of pain, but saying to himself, " What do I care ; a new limb will soon come out!" for among the crustaceæ such is the case—a new limb soon springs out, and takes the place of the one lost; so I was left without my prize. The women again warned me to be very careful, instructing me how to catch crabs by seizing the big claw and severing it from the body ; but, before doing this, the stick must be placed on the middle of the back, where the claws can not reach, as they can not move backward.

I soon spied another crab, but he heard my footstep, and with the utmost speed made for his burrow. Then I came suddenly upon another, just in front of me; he had not time to turn round ; so, shoving my stick in front of him until it nearly touched his two big eyes, I put him into a furious rage. By-and-by he managed to seize the stick, which he shook, just as the other crab had done my finger. I was thankful that it was not my finger this time. The motion of the claw at the junction with the body was very queer. After some trouble, I managed to secure this fellow. Then I went after another, which at once took to his burrow and disappeared; but I was determined to watch and wait for him. I noticed him every now and then peering slyly out, drawing in his head at the slightest noise; so I hid behind his burrow, and kept very still. At last he came out, walking slowly from his hole. I put my foot on his burrow, upon which he turned round, and ran one way and then another, and finally made for another burrow, where he met the possessor coming out from his "castle," when a general fight of claws ensued. The aggressor, being the stronger, succeeded in winning the battle and getting in, while the other, in his fright, plunged into a burrow the owner of which had probably been killed that morning.

Great slaughter of the crabs had already taken place, and so many heavy, fat fellows had been captured that we were sure of a great feast. It was well for us that it was so, for at last the ogombons got thoroughly frightened and remained in their burrows; not one was to be seen; so, after having captured some thousands of them, we got back into our canoes and ascended the river again.

The ogombons are peculiar. I think they never go to the sea, but deposit their eggs on the shores of the island, for I never met them on the sea-coast. They feed on all kinds of refuse, on black mud, leaves, berries, etc., etc. The crabs found on the main land are not eaten, the natives believing that they sometimes visit their cemeteries. On the white sand of the sea-shore are found innumerable little crabs of the same color as the sand itself.

Besides the ogombons there are many other land-crabs, but they are much smaller, and are not eaten by the natives. Many of these crabs are of the most gorgeous colors, some purple and red, others blue and red; they are exceedingly wild, and swift of foot. They live close to the sea, and may be seen on the shore in great numbers during the night.

I wish I had had time to spare to study these crabs more thoroughly than I have done, but I have told you the little I know about them.

As we returned we had to pass through the midst of the tremendous herd of hippopotami which I have mentioned. For years that herd had taken possession of an immense mud-bank lying between the island and the main land, or rather the tongue of land which separated the sea from the River Fernand Vaz.

The hippopotami began to grunt, and plunged into the water, remaining there for some time, and then would come again to the surface, until gradually the navigation became dangerous, so much so that we had to be very careful, and paddle along the shore for fear of being upset by these huge creatures, who would surge from under the water in every direction, and we knew not where the next one would rise. Two or three times one rose very near my canoe. I did not want to fire at them, for they would have sunk to the bottom, and would not have risen for two or three days after, and then probably they would have been found at the mouth of the river, or been driven into the sea by the current. By the kind of groan or hoarse grunt they gave, I made up my mind that they were becoming enraged at having been disturbed, so we paddled carefully on until I thought we were at last out of their reach. But we were to receive a good fright before we had done with them, for I saw a canoe just ahead of the one in which I was seated rocking and jerking about in an extraordinary manner, and the people in it shouting at the top of their voices, and there came up a huge hippopotamus, which gave a terrific grunt, immediately responded to by the other hippopotami we had left behind. We paddled hard in order to get out of the way, for the huge creature seemed to be maddened; and at last, with a thankful heart, I left all the hippopotami behind, and, after some severe paddling, we reached a safe place on the bank of the river, where a general and grand cooking of the crabs began.

CHAPTER XII.

STRANGE SPIDERS.—THE HOUSE-SPIDER.—HOW THEY CAPTURE THEIR PREY.—HOW THEY FIGHT.—FIGHT BETWEEN A WASP AND A SPIDER.—THE SPIDER HAS ITS LEGS CUT OFF, AND IS CARRIED AWAY.—BURROW SPIDER WATCHING FOR ITS PREY.

Now I must pause a little in that great jungle, and recount to you some of the queer things which I have seen among the spiders—the burrowing spiders, the house-spiders, the wall-spiders, and the spiders which weave their big and far-spreading webs among the trees of the forest or the tall grass of the open fields. I hope you will feel as interested as I did when you learn how smart many of them are.

There are a very great variety of spiders in the country I have explored. Some are of queer shape. Each species has its peculiar habits. I often wish I had devoted more of my time to the study of their habits, and to ascertaining the way in which they catch their prey; but what I have observed I will relate to you. I will speak to you first of the house-spiders, and what I saw of them.

In many of the little huts where I lived, the walls of which were made of the bark of trees, there were always several house-spiders, which I took good care not to kill, for they were seemingly inoffensive, only they were great enemies to the cockroaches, insects, and flies. Sometimes in the evening, when I laid down on my acoco (bed of sticks), by the light of a torch my eyes would rest upon the wall, and I would see emerging from some crack a queer-looking gray spider, and now and then cockroaches, which swarm in the African huts, or some other kind of insect, would come out on the walls. Then the spider would slyly advance toward the insect, taking great care to approach it from behind, in order not to be seen by the unsuspecting victim, with which it is soon to engage in a deadly struggle, for the spider is brave and voracious, and is not to be easily frightened by the size of its antagonist.

These house-spiders are of a dull gray, which color assists in concealing its approach. After leaving its lair and getting a good position, it remains perfectly rigid and motionless, often for half an hour, waiting for some unlucky cockroach to pass by. At last the cockroach rushes past. In an instant the spider, with great impetuosity, pounces upon him. Then ensues a tug and a battle which is of great interest—a conflict for life on the part of the cockroach, a combat for food on the part of the spider, which for the time seems more voracious and ferocious than a tiger or leopard. The battle is often prolonged for more than half an hour. The great black African cockroach grows to a large size, and is a very strong and formidable opponent for the spider. The latter, after pouncing on its victim, fastens on its back, and, to prevent being borne off, clings with two of his hairy hind legs, which seem to have little hooks, to the floor or to the wall. All the cockroach's endeavors and frantic exertions are to escape. He tugs and jerks, and generally succeeds at first in dragging its enemy off for some distance. The desperate struggle goes on, the spider using all its power and strength. It manages again to get a hold with its feet. At last it succeeds in fastening its head on the body of the cockroach, and begins sucking away at the juices of the latter, which, at the pain of the first bite, makes the greatest efforts to escape, for it knows that the deadly struggle has begun. Then there would be a tremendous fight. I sometimes thought the cockroach would escape, both being exhausted. Then would come a pause. Presently the struggle would recommence, the spider sucking away all the time, and the poor cockroach at last succumbing, whereupon his enemy drags off the body to some corner or hiding-place where it can be devoured at leisure.

Once in the daytime, a few days after seeing the fight I have been describing to you, I saw the same spider, for I knew its place of hiding, come out after an insect. It was creeping slowly toward its prey, when a wasp—one of those beautiful, long-legged, and slender wasps, with striped bodies, which are so common here—came to attack the spider. Quickly she flew over the spider, her long legs hanging down and plying between the legs of the poor spider, who was now in as bad a plight as the cockroach was a few days before. In this latter case, cunning instead of strength was to be used.

The wasp kept flying above the spider, moving her long legs with great rapidity between the legs of the spider, while her head was touching that of her opponent, and giving a bite from time to time. Then the spider tried to run away, but could not, for the long legs of the wasp moved between his legs in a backward sort of a way, which prevented the spider from advancing. The wasp all the time was hovering above the spider with very quick motions, her legs moving so fast that I could not see all their movements. Suddenly the wasp turned round, and put her head down close to the right front leg of the spider, to which it gave one or two bites, just where it is joined to the body, and the leg dropped down; then she worked away at the head for a few seconds, then again turned round and gave a bite or two to the leg next to the one that had just been cut, and this dropped down also. I had never seen any thing fly so fast. At last the poor spider seemed perfectly stunned; he could hardly move. I considered the fight over, and that the wasp was victor. Another leg dropped down, and then another, all being cut just where they are attached to the body, till at last they were all cut down. When the last hind leg dropped, the wasp seized the body of the spider, and flew away outside of my little hut to devour it.

I missed my spider very much afterwards, and the cockroaches had their own way for a few days without fear of being devoured, till another house-spider made its appearance.

In one of my little huts there were other species of spider besides the one I have spoken to you about, whose little webs would be built in places where they would be most apt to entangle the flies. After these had been caught, the spider would immediately come out and suck their blood. However small the fly might be, the spider would come, and even when only a musquito had been taken, it would come, but it would give only one or two sucks, and then would go away. You will agree that there must be very little to suck out of a musquito that has not been feeding on a human being.

In the tall grass which sometimes grows round the

E

village, or in the large open spaces where trees have been cut down, there is found a tremendous big bright yellow and black spider, whose web spreads over a space of several feet, and so thick and strong is it that, when I have got entangled in one, I could certainly feel a slight impediment to my walk, or the moving of my arm. The threads of the web are yellow, the same color as one part of the spider. This spider belongs probably to the genus Mygale. Some of them grow to be of immense size; I have frequently seen them with a body as large as a sparrow's egg.

Happily, the bite of this spider is not dangerous, for one day, as I was pursuing a bird and was in the midst of a lot of grass, the blades of which stuck to my skin and cut me like a razor, and I was watching and pursuing the bird in order not to lose sight of it, I got entangled in one of these big webs—by far the biggest web built by any spider I have ever heard of. I looked round to see and get out of the spider's way, but before I was aware I got a bite which was almost as painful as the sting of a scorpion. In my fright I tumbled down. I had no ammonia with me, consequently I returned at once to the village, where I had some, but by the time I reached home I felt no ill effect, the pain having left me a few minutes after the bite.

These big spiders are said by the natives to make these large, spreading webs in order to catch little birds, the blood of which they suck. I never saw a bird caught, nor even any remains of feathers in the web, but from the strength of the web I am certain that many little birds, if once caught, could not get out, and that this big spider is fully equal to mastering little birds, for its

BIT BY A SPIDER.

strength must be very great if it is as strong in proportion to its size as other spiders are.

At any rate, if birds are caught in their webs, it must be very seldom. But if their webs do not catch birds, they are tremendous traps for flies, wasps, beetles, and insects of all kinds; for I have never long watched one of them without seeing some living thing of one kind or another caught, and then immediately the big, long-legged spider would come swiftly and suck the blood of the victim; two or three suckings would finish up a common black fly. They are very voracious, and attack the prey with great vigor.

They must like the powerful sun, for many of their webs are built in the open spaces where Master Sol has his own way. The rain can not incommode them as he does us.

When one of these webs is finished it will remain perfect a long time; sometimes it will stand for months before the owner begins to make another.

One day in the forest I spied not far from the ground, just by an old dead tree, a little bit of a long-legged spider waging a terrible conflict with a caterpillar, which, without exaggeration, must have been at least thirty or forty times larger than the body of the little, slender, and long-legged spider. I immediately took from my pocket my magnifying-glass, in order to see better; then saw, about four inches from the ground, spreading from under the dead branch of the tree, several threads of a web which hung down, embracing a space of four or five inches, and ending in one thread as it came near the caterpillar. That single thread was entangled in the hair of the caterpillar and round its neck, and the caterpillar hung by it. The end of his body scarcely touched the ground. Then there was a desperate struggle. I suppose the caterpillar, before being caught, was down on the ground quietly eating some leaves, and the spider dropped down upon it like a wild beast would pounce upon its prey.

I lay flat on the ground to look at the conflict. This time the long legs of the spider were of the same use to it as were those of the wasp in the other fight I have related.

For a long while there was a great struggle, the caterpillar shaking and turning round and round as it hung by that single thread; often its body would twist into a circle, the end touching the head, when suddenly, at one of these twists, the spider, by some dexterous movements, spun one of its threads round the caterpillar, binding the tail to the head. The caterpillar, by a desperate effort, broke the thread, and freed the lower part of its body. The spider was so small that I had to use the magnifying-glass all the time in order to watch its movements. At first the attention of the spider was entirely engaged in securing its prey. When the caterpillar was struggling hard to disentangle itself, it would come down and spin thread after thread round the hairy body of its victim, and then unite them to the single thread.

Now and then, with its pincers, which appeared through the magnifying-glass to be very large in comparison with the size of the body, it would try to cut the large pincers of the caterpillar. The end of its long legs, as they came round the head and eyes of the caterpillar, seemed to annoy it terribly, to judge by the struggles of the worm. At last the spider succeeded in seizing the base of the right pincer of the caterpillar, and tried to cut it, but in vain. In less than fifteen seconds it returned to the task, and went at the left pincer, with apparently no better success. Then, after a while, its attacks were directed to a spot between the pincers. He kept at it and kept at it, apparently sucking the blood, till finally, after thirty-seven minutes of deadly conflict, the caterpillar, a mammoth in comparison with the size of the spider, hung dead. Then the spider finished sucking the blood of its victim. While the spider was carrying on this deadly combat, it did not mind me when I touched its web with a little stick: it would just ascend the single thread by which it was suspended, and then, within a few seconds, would return to the fight. After the caterpillar had been killed, when I touched the web it would go up, and remain there for a long time—three or four minutes—before it came down. Finally I took hold of the caterpillar; down came the spider, and with him part of his web. The spider ran along the ground for a few inches, then suddenly rolled itself into a ball and lay apparently dead, the legs being twisted round the body. It appeared to me that the spider thought a wasp was going to attack it, and thus protected itself.

After a little while I came to look at the poor dead caterpillar, and saw a few ants hard at work carrying it off somewhere to be devoured.

Among the great many species of spiders there are some which are very curious. Among the most remarkable are those which burrow holes in the ground and live in them. These ground-spiders are short, and have powerful fangs and legs.

Several species of spiders have short legs, and flat, oval bodies, surrounded by pointed spurs, looking, when taken from their webs, more like bugs than veritable spiders.

The cave in which the burrow spiders live is but a few inches long, built in the shape of a tube, from the opening of which they watch for their prey. The interior of the burrow is like felt, and is so arranged that it forms a tunnel that prevents the earth from falling in.

Some of the burrow spiders are called trap-door spiders, on account of the curious way in which the entrance of their abode is guarded. A trap-door closes the entrance. This door is made of the same material as the interior of the tube, to which it is attached by a kind of hinge, by which it falls squarely upon it. This trap-door is made to protect the spider from its enemies, among which are wasps and many species of ants. These latter sometimes make short work of a spider.

This door is a marvel; the outside is generally covered with earth similar in color to the ground by which it is surrounded, thus rendering it difficult to find the burrow.

Trap-door spiders are found in many parts of the world.

But many species of spiders live in burrows that have no doors.

Some of these burrow spiders go out at night as well as in the daytime, but they hardly ever move far from their burrows. I have often seen them watching from the entrance of their caves for prey. How queer they look! They must have a wonderful sense of hearing, for at the least noise they run back inside of their burrows. They seem to know when the noise does not come from an enemy, but from some insect upon which they intend to prey. One day one of these burrow spiders was watching for its food, when suddenly it pounced upon a big caterpillar which had made its appearance; and, after a desperate struggle, the poor caterpillar was carried into the burrow, though still alive.

After half an hour I carefully demolished the burrow, and found the spider at the bottom; the caterpillar was partly devoured, and I saw the remains of legs, wings, and heads of insects which had been captured and eaten up. I took the spider out; it seemed stupefied, and walked to and fro as if it did not know where to go.

When once a spider has built its burrow it dwells in it

for a long time. These burrows are built in such a manner that when it rains the water can not get in.

Have you ever thought, when looking at the web of a spider, what an admirable piece of work it is, and how this thread is manufactured? No lace is more beautifully worked. The thread is formed by a semi-liquid secretion, which comes out, at the will of the spider, through minute apertures, and which hardens into a thread by contact with the atmosphere.

How strange that is!

Spiders must have a great amount of knowledge, and are, no doubt, good barometers, for when a storm is impending they never will build or mend a web. There is a good reason for their not being extravagant in the use of their silk, for, although they can use at their will the secretion from which the thread is made, it requires time to reproduce it; so when you see a spider spinning new webs, it is a sign of fine weather coming.

If you look closely at the web of a spider, you will surely be surprised at their wonderful skill. First a net-work of strong threads is built; these are the main beams, and between them the net made of smaller thread is spun. These webs are exceedingly elastic, for they have to resist the power of the wind. When the web has been long built, and has become stretched, they will sometimes go and fetch a little piece of wood, which they hang by a thread, and haul it to a spot where they think it will steady their structure.

The threads of spiders are produced from an organ called the "spinneret," which is placed at the extremity of the body. The spinnerets are arranged in pairs, and are four, six, or eight in number.

The spider generally works at its web with its head down, lowering itself by its thread. The whole is worked by the sense of touch, the threads being guided by one of the hind legs. If you take the trouble to watch a spider working, you will see it work just as I have described.

The semi-liquid secretion is forced out through very small apertures, which may be called miniature tubes; they look very much like very minute hairs. These tubes cover the spinnerets, which are externally like little rounded projections, but their shape is not always the same. The threads become quite strong, for after leaving the tubes they are united together, and hence are much stronger than if the thread was composed of a single strand.

E 2

CHAPTER XIII.

WE CONTINUE OUR WANDERINGS.—JOINED BY ETIA.—WE STARVE.—GAMBO AND ETIA GO IN SEARCH OF BERRIES.—A HERD OF ELEPHANTS.—THE ROGUE ELEPHANT CHARGES ME.—HE IS KILLED.—HE TUMBLES DOWN NEAR ME.—STORY OF REDJIOUA.

Now we have left the land-crabs and the spiders, let us continue our wanderings in the jungle. I am ransacking the forest to discover and understand all that is in it. We had a lot of fun at that time. I was in good health and spirits. I was perhaps a little reckless, and did not seem to care for any thing. When there was danger in an undertaking, I frequently did not think enough about it, but rather took delight in it, scorpions, centipedes, and venomous serpents being the exception, for I rather objected to them, and did not fancy meeting them in my hunt, or under my bed, nor, indeed, any where else. Whenever I could, I killed them without mercy.

I delighted to sleep under the trees, in the midst of the thickest part of the forest, and where savage beasts were plentiful. In that case I always kept a sharp lookout, and saw that our fires were kept blazing.

Friend Etia had come to meet us, and was going to join us in the woods for a few days, and we were all glad to see him. One day, while we were hunting, we came to a spot where large quantities of fern were growing under the tall trees, and we saw that in the morning a large herd of elephants had been there, for their heavy footprints were strongly marked on the ground. Immediately there was great rejoicing, for we knew that the elephants could not be far off.

How eager were the faces of Malaouen, Querlaouen, and Gambo. They looked at their guns as if to say, " I hope you will help me to kill an elephant." The guns I gave them were their great pets.

Gambo and Etia had gone away through the jungle, and were to remain two days collecting berries and nuts, and then they were to come back to us. We were in a sorry plight—we were starving. We could not wait for them, for fear that, while waiting, the elephants would move off. What a pity! each of us might bag an elephant. By the way, should I say bag? When I was a boy I used to bag squirrel; that is to say, put them in my bag.

It was about three o'clock when we came upon the tracks of the elephants. What a number of them must be together! "There must be at least twenty," whispered Malaouen. "There must be at least thirty," said Querlaouen. Malaouen insisted there were only twenty. Then I had my say, and I said I thought there were about twenty-five. We tracked them till five o'clock, and then concluded that we had better have our camp built where we were, rather than go too near to them.

Being the dry season, we were not afraid of rain or tornadoes, so we chose a place to lie down, under a gigantic tree, as there we would only require a fire in front of us, our backs being protected by the tree, and the leopards would have less chance at us, and we would not have to build so many fires.

In the evening we furbished our guns, chose the steel-pointed bullets we used for elephants, and then went to sleep on the dry ground.

During the night we were awakened by a tremendous crashing of trees all round us, and we saw elephants bounding in the forest like wild bulls, tearing every thing before them, and then disappearing through the darkness. They seemed perfectly mad.

Malaouen shouted, "Chaillie! the bashikouays are coming; let us make a big fire. He had hardly said this when I heard the tremendous roar of a male gorilla, then the piercing shrieks of his female, followed by the cries of a young gorilla.

We immediately scattered the fire-wood we had lighted. It was high time, for the bashikouay were coming. The insects began flying over our heads. Happily, we were in the midst of a fortress of fire.

In less than half an hour they had gone on their march, and the forest became as silent as the night itself.

We had had a narrow escape. If it had not been for the timely warning of the elephants, we should have been obliged to clear out double-quick through that jungle in the middle of the night. It would have been no joke.

"The bashikouay have driven away every thing before them. What will become of our elephants?" I said. "They may have gone a great distance, and it may take us five days to overtake them. I wish the bashikouay had gone somewhere else."

We went to sleep again, and when we awoke it was broad daylight. The birds were singing, and the sun's rays peeped through the dark foliage.

I was really annoyed, for I was sure the elephants had

gone a long way off. We could not pursue them, I thought, for it would take so much time that Etia and Gambo might return and not find us. Then Malaouen said that the elephants had probably gone back among the ferns, and we had better try to find them there. He was not mistaken, for when we went back there we saw at once that their footsteps were in that direction.

We traveled slowly in the dense jungle, now and then frightening a guinea-fowl. At other times we would see a snake running away before us, or we would meet a strange insect or a queer butterfly. Malaouen, who this time walked ahead of me, suddenly turned round and made me a sign to stop, and then he came near me, his feet appearing not to touch the ground; I could not hear them. He whispered to me the word *njogoo* (elephant). I started, I looked round, I could not see any, and I could not understand how Malaouen could have seen them. His quick ear had heard the sound of the footsteps of one. We advanced carefully. At last I saw the elephants lying quietly on the ground. I counted twenty of the huge beasts, and among them I recognized a tremendous bull elephant. What a sight it was! On a sudden the elephants got up, and they all retreated slowly through the forest, with the exception of the old bull, who stood still. I think I still see him, with his long ears, his big tusks, his thick, wrinkled black skin, covered with scattered and short hair. Malaouen and I lay flat on the ground, as flat as we possibly could. It was no child's play. We were to have a little business to transact with the bull, the fighting one of the herd. If we missed him he would charge us, and, what made it worse, we could not get a good shot at the huge and leviathan-like creature. Presently Malaouen crawled forward; I lay still. How he could crawl without making a noise I could not tell, but he did it, till at last he almost came under the elephant's body. The elephant was looking toward me, and Malaouen had succeeded in approaching from behind. I was thinking that if Malaouen did not kill the elephant where he stood, I would run the risk of being charged by him and trampled to death, unless I shot the beast dead upon the spot. I felt like shouting to Malaouen to be careful, and not to miss his shot at the elephant. When his gun rose, it rose slowly but surely; then I heard a tremendous detonation, and down the elephant came in my direction, close upon me. I fired, and the monster fell just in front of where I was lying. Three or four yards more, and he would have tumbled down upon me, and probably made a pancake of your friend. Querlaouen came rushing to the rescue, but the great beast lay without motion. Querlaouen had killed him. I had shot the elephant right between the two eyes, which is not a good spot, while Querlaouen's bullet had gone right into his body through the lower part of the belly.

We looked like ants by the side of that huge creature. We cut his tail off, and then returned to our old camp, which was not far distant, where we were to meet Etia and Gambo.

In the afternoon they came in, and when we showed them the elephant's tail they looked at us with amazement, as if they did not believe their own eyes. Then they shouted, "You are men! you are men!" They were loaded with wild nuts, and thus we were to have plenty of food!

DEATH OF THE BULL ELEPHANT.

In despite of my best endeavors to prevent it, there must be some heathen ceremonies to celebrate our victory over the elephant.

The hind quarters were cut off, and, with a piece of the flesh, were set apart and carried into the forest for the spirit Alombo to feed upon. Then my men muttered some words that I could not understand, but I did not care, for we were very much like the man who, when traveling in India, received an elephant as a present, and did not know what to do with it.

The next day, after taking as much elephant meat as we could, we moved away, for the flies were coming pretty thick; and besides, the bashikouay might return again, and the smell would not be of the pleasantest after a couple of days' sojourn by the body of the dead elephant.

So we started for another part of the forest, and built our camp several miles farther to the north of the place where we had been. Of course we chose a spot where there was a beautiful little stream, so that we had plenty of good water to drink. The next morning we were to go hunting, and we were glad to be all together again, it was so nice. We busied ourselves smoking our elephant meat, so that we might be sure of having food for a good many days, though we should not find any berries.

We furbished our guns, and had a real nice day in getting ready for some grand hunting. Nothing during the night disturbed us, and the next morning we all felt strong and refreshed. Querlaouen and I went hunting together, while Malaouen and Gambo went off in another direction.

We were really lost in that great jungle, and yet we

appeared to think that the forest belonged to us. We were to come back toward sundown; no one was to camp out by himself. That was the law I made that day. The country was hilly, and under the tall trees the ground was covered with a dense jungle. That day nothing was seen, and toward night we were glad to rest our weary limbs by the huge pile of blazing fire, and then we went to sleep, hoping to be more fortunate the next time. Our supper was composed of a few wild berries, but chiefly of elephant meat, my men enjoying the elephant marvelously. After our supper, and before we went to sleep, Querlaouen got up and said, "Now I am going to tell you a story."

REDJIOUA, A KING.—AKENDA MBANI.

"Long ago, long before our fathers lived, in a far country there lived a king called Redjioua. That king had a daughter called Arondo. Arondo (sweetheart) was beautiful—more beautiful than all the girls of the country. Redjioua said to the people, 'Though a man would ask my daughter in marriage, and present me with a great many slaves, goats, and tusks of ivory, so that he might "soften" my heart to have her, he can not have her. I want only a man that shall agree that, when Arondo will be ill, he must be ill also; that when Arondo dies, he must die also the same day.'

"Years passed by; no one came to ask Arondo in marriage, for all were afraid of the law the king had made, no one being willing to die when she died."

I questioned Querlaouen, "Did Arondo ever marry?"

"Wait a little while and you will hear," said friend Querlaouen, as gently as he could.

"There was a man in that country called Akenda Mbani (never goes twice to the same place)." Many names among the tribes of Equatorial Africa have a meaning, and remember that Akenda Mbani's means "Never goes twice to the same place."

"Akenda Mbani came to the king and said to him, 'I come to marry Arondo, your daughter, the one you have (*tená coni*) made a law concerning; so I have brought no ivory, or slaves, or goats. I come without the things, for I agree to die when Arondo dies.'

"So Redjioua gave his beautiful daughter, the pride of his heart, the loveliest woman of his dominion, to Akenda Mbani.

"Akenda Mbani was a great hunter, but, as his name implied, he never went twice to the same place in the forest to hunt. But his name did not prevent his moving about his own village.

"After he had married Arondo, he went hunting, and one day he killed two wild boars, after which exploit he returned to the village of his father-in-law, carrying one of the boars on his back. He went to Redjioua and said, 'Father, I have killed two wild boars; I bring you one.' The king said, 'Thank you, my son; go and fetch the other.' Then Akenda Mbani replied, 'When I was born, my father, in giving me my name of Akenda Mbani, gave me a coni (a law) never to go twice to the same place.' So the other wild boar was lost, as no one could tell where it was to be found in the forest.

"Then he went hunting again, and killed two antelopes. Of course Akenda Mbani said he could not go and fetch the other."

Then Gambo interrupted the story by saying, "The

king knew very well that Akenda Mbani could not go twice to the same spot; why did he ask him to go?"

"I can not say why," said Querlaouen; "I tell you the story as it has come to us from our forefathers."

"Shortly afterward Akenda Mbani killed two beautiful *bongos*, and brought one back. Then the people came and asked him to show them the way, so they might fetch the other. But Akenda Mbani said, 'You know that if we do not keep the coni our father gave us, we are sure to die. I do not wish to die for a bongo, so I can not go.' He thus went shooting month after month, but would never go back to the same spot.

"One fine evening, as Akenda Mbani was seated in front of his house, the people came to him and said, 'A people called Oroungous have come; they have come to trade, and also to buy ten slaves.'

"Akenda Mbani turned to his wife and said, 'Let us go and meet the Oroungous, who are still in their canoe on the river-bank, and who have come to be my guests.'

"Then they went and met the Oroungous. Akenda Mbani took a chest of goods, and put the chest on the head of his wife, and he himself took a sword, and they returned to their home, leaving the Oroungous on the beach.

"A moon (month) passed away since the Oroungous had left, and the chest which the Oroungous had brought, and which Arondo carried to her house, had not been opened. One evening Arondo said to her husband, 'Let us go and see what is in the chest.' So they went and took the cover off, and inside they discovered the most beautiful things, that had come from the white man's country. The chest was quite full of beautiful cloths.

Arondo desired her husband to take two fathoms of one beautiful cloth, as she liked it. So Akenda Mbani cut off two fathoms. The chest was then closed again, and they left the place.

"Then Akenda Mbani seated himself on an *ebongo* (stool), and Arondo on the *acoco* (bed), and she began to sew. She had only pierced the cloth four times with her needle when she exclaimed, 'Husband! husband! I begin to have a headache!' Akenda Mbani replied, 'Take care, take care. Do not be sick if you do not wish me to die;' and he looked her steadily in the face. Arondo called again, 'Akenda Mbani! Akenda Mbani! my husband, do tie a string round my head, for I have a great deal of pain.' Then Arondo tied a string round her husband's head also, though he had no headache.

"In a short time Arondo began to cry again, for she suffered greatly, and her headache was getting worse and worse. Akenda Mbani was becoming frightened, for he did not want to die.

"The news of Arondo's illness spread all over the village, and soon reached the ears of King Redjioua, her father. The whole people of the village came to see Arondo, and many were around her when she was crying and calling on her father. The king said, 'Do not cry, my daughter; you will not die, my child.' As soon as Arondo heard this, she moaned, 'Ah father! ah father! why did you say I will not die, for you know that if you *daga* (mourn, lament, fear) death it is sure to come.'

She had hardly uttered these words when she died. The people mourned and wept, putting their hands over their heads.

"Redjioua said, 'As my daughter is dead, Akenda

Mbani must die also.' Akenda Mbani answered, 'I will die, that I may be buried with Arondo, my wife.' So Akenda was killed.

"The king ordered a slave to be buried alive with his daughter. There were also placed in her grave ten dishes, ten jars full of palm wine, ten baskets, ten tusks of ivory, and many other things, among which was the chest of the Oroungous."

There was a dead silence among us all, for we wanted to hear the end of the story. Querlaouen stopped for breath, and then continued:

"The place where the people are buried is called Ndjimai, and here they laid the bodies of Akenda Mbani and of Arondo, side by side in one grave, laying over them the spears of Akenda Mbani, his battle-axe, the bed upon which he and his wife had slept, his cutlasses, and his hunting-bag. Then the people said, 'Now let us cover the grave with sand,' which they did until a little mound was formed.

"Then Agambouai (this name means the speaker of the village) said, 'King, there are leopards here.' As soon as Redjioua heard this, he cried, 'Do not build a mound over the grave of my child, for fear that leopards may see it, scratch up the earth, and eat the body of my beautiful daughter.'

"They replied, 'Let us take the things back and dig a deeper grave.' Then they took away the things, and seated the bodies of Arondo and Akenda Mbani on two seats. When they had finished their work, and thought the grave deep enough, they replaced all the things they had taken out. Then they lifted the body of Arondo and laid her gently in the grave. Next they took hold of Akenda Mbani, and raised him gently to place him by the side of his wife; but he opened his eyes and mouth, and said, 'Don't you know I never go twice to the same place? If any of you attempt to place me again in the tomb, I will kill him, for you know I NEVER GO TWICE TO THE SAME PLACE.'

"He then rose, and, accompanied by the people, returned to the village; and when Redjioua saw him he said, 'How is it that Akenda Mbani has returned? I thought he had been killed and buried.'

"Up to the time of Redjioua, when a husband or wife died, the survivor was killed; but Akenda Mbani broke the law by rising again from the grave. Since then, no one is killed on account of the spouse dying."

From this legend, which has been handed down from generation to generation, I conclude that perhaps at a remote period it was compulsory for both husband and wife to die at the same time.

After a hearty laugh at the lucky escape of Akenda Mbani, my men thanked their stars that they were not born at that time, and then we all went to sleep.

CHAPTER XIV.

A FORMIDABLE BIRD.—THE PEOPLE ARE AFRAID OF IT.—A BABY CARRIED OFF BY THE GUANIONIEN.—A MONKEY ALSO SEIZED.—I DISCOVER A GUANIONIEN NEST.—I WATCH FOR THE EAGLES.

SEVERAL weeks have passed away since the story of Akenda Mbani was told us, and we have since been wandering through the forest in the midst of the intricate hunting-paths which Querlaouen knew so well. At night we would all meet and recount the adventures of the day, and eat the game which some of us had been fortunate enough to kill. In case we had killed no game, then we had our elephant meat to fall back upon.

How silent the forest was! Not a human being besides ourselves was to be seen. A leaf falling, a bird singing, a wild guinea-fowl calling for its mate, the footsteps of a gazelle, the chatter of a monkey, the hum of a bee, the rippling of the water of some beautiful little stream as it meandered through the forest, were the only noises that ever disturbed the stillness of this grand solitude.

Now and then we could hear the wind whispering strangely as it passed gently amid the branches of the tall trees hanging over our heads.

We must have looked strange indeed as we wandered through that great forest, where God alone could see us.

How strange every thing seemed to me! I was in another world, and novel objects every where met my eyes.

One morning I hear a strange cry high up in the air. I look, and what do I see?—what do I see yonder up in the sky? An eagle. But what kind of an eagle? for it appears to me so much larger than any eagle I have ever met with before. And as I asked this, my men exclaimed, "It is a *guanionien;* the leopard of the air; the bird that feeds on gazelles, goats, and monkeys; the bird that is the most difficult of any to find and to kill." "Yes," said Querlaouen; "in my younger days I remember that my wife and myself were on our plantation, with some of our slaves, and one day we heard the cries of a baby, and saw a child carried up into the sky by one of these guanioniens. The baby had been laid on the ground, and the guanionien, whose eyes never miss any thing, and which had not been noticed soaring above our heads, pounced on its prey, and then laughed at us as he rose and flew to a distant part of the forest." Then Querlaouen showed me a fetich partly made of two huge claws of this bird. What tremendous things those talons were! how deep they could go into the flesh!

Then came wonderful stories of the very great strength of the bird.

The people were afraid of them, and were compelled to be very careful of their babies. These grand eagles do not feed on fowls; they are too small game for them. Monkeys are what they like best; they can watch them as they float over the top of the trees of the forest; but sometimes the monkeys get the better of them.

"People had better not try to get hold of the guanionien's young if they want to keep their sight," said Gambo; "for, as sure as we live, the old bird will pounce upon the man that touches its young."

For a long time I had heard the people talking of the guanionien, but had never yet had a glimpse of one.

Now, looking up again, I saw several of them. How high they were! At times they would appear to be quite still in the air; at other times they would soar. They were so high that I do not see how they could possibly see the trees; every thing must have been in a haze to them; monkeys, of course, could not be seen. They were, no doubt, amusing themselves, and I wonder if they tried to see how near they could go to the sun. Some at times flew so high that I lost sight of them.

Oh, how I longed to kill a guanionien; but I never was able to do it. Once I examined one, but it was dead, and had been killed by spears as it had come down and seized a goat. The natives had kept it for me; but when I returned to the village it was quite spoiled and decomposed, the feathers having dropped out.

Several times I was on the point of killing one, but never was in time.

My men went hunting that morning, while I remained alone in the camp, for I felt tired, and wanted to write up my journal, and to describe all the things I had seen or heard during the past few days.

In the afternoon I thought I would ramble round. I took a double-barreled smooth-bore gun, and loaded one side with a bullet in case I should see large game; the other barrel I loaded with shot No. 2. Then I carefully plunged into the woods till I reached the banks of a little stream, and there I heard the cry of the mondi (*Colobus Satanus*), which is one of the largest monkeys of these forests. From their shrill cries, I thought there must be at least half a dozen together. I was indeed glad that I had one barrel loaded with big shot. If the mondis were not too far off, I would be able to get a fair shot, and kill one.

I advanced very cautiously until I got quite near to them. I could then see their big bodies, long tails, and long, jet-black, shining hair. What handsome beasts they were! what a nice-looking muff their skins would make! I thought.

Just as I was considering which of them I would fire at, I saw some big thing, like a large shadow, suddenly come down upon the tree. Then I heard the flapping of heavy wings, and also the death-cry of a poor mondi. Then I saw a huge bird, with a breast spotted somewhat like a leopard, raise itself slowly into the air, carrying the monkey in its powerful finger-like talons. The claws of one leg were fast in the upper part of the neck of the monkey; so deep were they in the flesh that they were completely buried, and a few drops of blood fell upon the leaves below. The other leg had its claws quite deep into the back of the monkey. The left leg was kept higher than the right, and I could see that the great strength of the bird was used at that time to keep the neck, and also the back of the victim, from moving. The bird rose higher and higher, the monkey's tail swayed to and fro, and then both disappeared. It was a guanionien. Its prey was, no doubt, taken to some big tree where it could be devoured.

The natives say that the first thing the guanionien does is to take out the eyes of the monkeys they catch. But there must be a fearful struggle, for these mondis are powerful beasts, and do not die at the eagle's will. There must be a great trial of strength; for if the monkey is not seized at an exact place on the neck, he can turn his head, and he then inflicts a fearful bite on the breast of the eagle, or on his neck or leg, which disables his most terrible enemy, and then both, falling, meet their death.

I looked on without firing. The monkeys seemed paralyzed with fear when the eagle came down upon them, and did not move until after the bird of prey had taken one of their number, and then decamped. When I looked for them they had fled for parts unknown to me in the forest. I was looking so intently at the eagle and its prey that for a while I had forgotten the mondis. I do not wonder at it, for monkeys I could see often, but it is only once in a great while that such a scene as I witnessed could be seen by a man. It was grand; and I wondered not that the natives called the guanionien the leopard of the air. As I write these lines, though several years have passed away, I see still before me that big, powerful bird carrying its prey to some unknown part of the forest.

Long after the time I have been speaking to you about, I was hunting in the forest, when I came to a spot where I saw on the ground more than a hundred skulls of various animals, and of monkeys of all sizes, from those of baby monkeys to those of large mandrills; and there were two or three skulls of young chimpanzees. What a ghastly sight it was! Some of these skulls seemed almost fresh; they were skulls of all the species of monkeys found in the forest.

What could all this mean? I quickly perceived that these skulls were all scattered round a huge tree which rose higher than any of the trees surrounding it. Raising my eyes toward the top, I saw a huge nest made of branches of trees. I looked and looked in vain. I could not even hear the cries of any young birds. They had gone; they must have left their nest, and I wondered if they would come back at night with the *old folks;* so I concluded that I would lie in wait.

I waited in vain. The sun set, and no guanionien; darkness came, and no guanionien. Then I took a box of matches from my hunting-bag, and set fire to a large pile of wood which I had made ready, and then I cooked a few plantains I had with me.

I was all alone; I had taken no one with me. How quiet and silent every thing was around me that night! Now and then I could hear the dew that had collected on the leaves above come down drop after drop. I could see a bright star through the thick foliage of the trees. I could hear the music of the musquitoes round me; for I think there is something musical about the buzzing of a musquito, though there is nothing pleasant about its bite. I could see now and then a beautiful and bright fire-fly, which seemed to be like a light flitting through the jungle from place to place, sometimes remaining still and giving a stream of light all round as it rested on some big leaves for a while, then moving farther on.

Now and then I could hear the mournful cry of the owl, and at times I fancied I could hear the footstep of wild beasts walking in the silence of night.

I did not sleep at all that night; I did not wish to do so; and, as I was seated by the fire, I thought of the strange life I had led for some time past—how strange every thing was from what I had been accustomed to see at home. There was not a tree in the forest that we had in ours, and the face of a white man had not been seen by me for a very long time.

The night passed slowly, but at last the cries of the partridges reminded me that daylight was not far off. When the twilight came, it was of very short duration; the birds began to sing, the insects to move about, the monkeys to chatter, but the hyena, the leopard, and other night-animals had retired long before the sunlight into their dens.

Then I got up and roasted a plantain, which I ate; forthwith I shouldered my gun and started back for the village by a hunting-path that I knew.

Coming to the banks of a stream, where the water was as pure and limpid as crystal, I seated myself by the charming rivulet, thinking I would refresh myself by taking a bath, when lo! what do I see? a large snake swimming in the water. Its body was black, and its belly yellow, with black stripes. I immediately got up and fired at the disgusting creature, which I killed; and that water, which appeared to me a few minutes before so nice, was, to my eyes, no longer so.

CHAPTER XV.

THE CASCADE OF NIAMA-BIEMBAI.—A NATIVE CAMP.—STARTING FOR THE HUNT.—A MAN ATTACKED BY A GORILLA.—HIS GUN BROKEN.—THE MAN DIES.—HIS BURIAL.

AFTER wandering through the forest, at times coming back to the Bakalai village for food, Gambo suggested that we should go and see his father, who was an Ashira chief, and who had built an olako in the forest not far from the Bakalai village of Ndjali-Coudie.

We traveled through the forest until we reached a beautiful cascade, called Niama-Biembai. How gracefully Niama-Biembai wanders through the hills, falling from rock to rock! Its bed is gravelly, and its water clear and pure, like some Northern brook. How I loved to look at Niama-Biembai, and, by the gentle noise its waters made in falling, to think of friends who were far away!

Just in sight of this charming cascade was the encampment of Gambo's father, whom I had met before. We were received with great joy by the people. The evening of my arrival the olako was busy with preparations. Meat was scarce—very scarce; *gouamba* (hunger for meat) had seized the people, and the great hunters were getting ready for the hunt, and the people were joyful in the belief that plenty of game would be brought into the camp.

In the evening the hunters spoke with hollow and sonorous voices, and called upon the spirits of their ancestors to protect them. They covered themselves with the chalk of the Alumbi, and then bled their hands.

Then we seated ourselves round the fire, and the eleven hunters who were going with me began to tell their wonderful stories.

The next morning we made for the hunting-paths. Seven men were to go off in one direction for gazelles, and three others, among whom I was one, were to hunt for gorillas. Malaouen and Querlaouen went by themselves; Gambo and another man accompanied me.

Before starting, Igoumba, the chief of the Olako, told us to be careful, for there were some bad and ferocious gorillas in the woods. After walking some distance, we finally made toward a dark valley, where Gambo said we should find our prey. We were soon in one of the most dense jungles I ever met in Africa. My poor pantaloons received several rents from the thorns; at last one of the legs was taken clean off, so I was left with one-leg pantaloons. We were at times in the midst of swamps, so this was one of the hardest days I had had for a long time.

The gorilla chooses the darkest and gloomiest forest for his home, and is found on the outskirts of the clearings only when in search of plantains, bananas, sugar-cane, or pine-apples. Often he chooses for his peculiar haunt a wood so dark that, even at midday, one can scarcely see ten yards. Oh young folks! I wish you could have been with me in some part of that great jungle, then you could have seen for yourselves.

Our little party had separated. My friends Malaouen and Querlaouen said they were going to seek for elephants.

Gambo, his friend, and myself were to hunt for gorillas. Gambo and I kept together; for really, if I had lost him, I should never have found my way back. All at once Gambo's friend left us, saying that he was going to a spot where the *tondo* (a fruit) was plentiful, and there might be gorillas there; so he went off.

He had been gone but a short time when I heard a gun fired only a little way from us, and then I heard the tremendous roar of the gorilla, which sounded like distant thunder along the sky. The whole forest seemed filled with the din. Oh how pale I must have looked! a cold shudder ran through me. When I looked at Gambo, his face looked anxious. We gazed in each other's faces without saying a word, but instinctively we made for the spot where we had heard the roar of the gorilla and detonation of the gun. When I first heard the gun I thought the gorilla had been slain, and my heart was filled with joy; but the joy was of short duration, for the roar immediately followed, to tell us that the gorilla was not dead.

Then through the forest resounded once more the crack of a gun, and immediately afterward the most terrific roars of the beast. He roared three times, and then all became silent; no more roars were heard, no more guns were fired. This time Gambo seized my arm in great agitation, and we hurried on, both filled with a dreadful and sickening alarm. We had not to go far before our worst fears were realized. We pressed through the jungle in search of our companion, and at last found him. The poor brave fellow, who had gone off alone, was lying on the ground in a pool of his own blood, and, I at first thought, quite dead. Beside him lay his gun;

the stock was broken, and the barrel bent almost double. In one place it was flattened, and it bore plainly the marks of the gorilla's teeth.

Yes; the huge monster, in his rage, had bitten the barrel of the gun, and his powerful teeth had gone fiercely into that piece of steel. What a face he must have made as he held the barrel of that gun between his tremendous teeth! how he must have gnashed them with rage! how the wrinkles on his old face must have shown out! It must have been one of the most horrid and frightful pictures that one could ever behold.

Lowering my body and putting my ear to his heart, I remained for a while pale and speechless. At last I discovered that his heart beat. Oh how glad I was!

I immediately tore to pieces the old shirt I wore—it was one of the last I possessed—and the remaining leg of my pantaloons, and began to dress his wounds. I never was much of a surgeon, so I felt somewhat awkward and nervous. Then I poured into his mouth a little brandy, which I took from the small flask I always carried with me in case of need, which revived him a little, and he was able, with great difficulty, to speak. And then he told us that he was walking in the jungle just where the tondo grew, when he suddenly met, face to face, a huge male gorilla. As soon as the gorilla saw him he was literally convulsed with rage, and rushed at him. It was a very gloomy part of the wood, and there were a great many barriers between him and the gorilla. It was almost quite dark in that thicket, but he took good aim, and fired at the beast when he was about eight yards off. The ball, he thought, had wounded him in the side. The monster at once began beating his breast, giving three most impressive roars, which shook the earth, and, with the greatest rage, advanced upon him.

To run away was impossible. He would have been caught by the muscular arm of the gorilla, and held in his powerful and giant hand, before he could have taken a dozen steps in the jungle. "So," said the poor fellow, "I stood my ground, and reloaded my gun as quickly as I could, for the gorilla was slowly but steadily advancing upon me. As I raised my gun to fire, the gorilla, which was quite close to me, stretched out his long and powerful arm, and dashed the gun from my grasp. It struck the ground with great violence and went off. Then, in an instant, and with a terrible roar, the animal raised his arm and came at me with terrific force. I was felled to the ground by a heavy blow from his immense open paw."

Here the poor fellow tried to raise his arm to his abdomen, and continued: "He cut me in two; and while I lay bleeding on the ground, the monster seized my gun, and I thought he would dash my brains out with it. That is all I remember. I know that I am going to die."

This huge gorilla thought the gun was his enemy, so he had seized it and dashed it on the ground, and then, not satisfied, had taken it up again and given it a tremendous bite—a bite which would have crushed the arm of a man more easily than we crush the bones of a young spring chicken.

The great strength of the gorilla seems to lie in that big, long, and gigantic muscular arm of his, and in his immense hands—which we may call paws—with which he strikes, the hand always being almost wide open as it strikes.

When we reached the spot the gorilla was gone, so Gambo blew his antelope-horn, calling upon the other men to rejoin us. We then made, with branches of trees, a kind of bed, laying lots of leaves over it, upon which we carried the poor fellow back to the camp of the Ashiras.

I still remember the heart-rending, piercing wail I heard when I entered the camp; how his poor wife came rushing out to meet him, holding his hand and crying, "Husband, do speak to me—do speak to me once more!" But he never spoke again, for at last his heart ceased to beat, and he was dead. He had been killed by a gorilla.

How sorry I was. I felt truly unhappy. They entreated me to give the poor fellow medicine. They seemed persuaded that I could prevent his dying; but I was far from my head-quarters, where all my medicines were, and I had nothing to suit his case.

The people declared, with one accord, that it was no true gorilla that had attacked him, but a man—a wicked man that had been turned into a gorilla. Such a being no one could escape, for he can not be killed.

The next morning I got up, and, taking my large bag, put into it provisions for three days, adding two or three pounds of powder, with forty or fifty large bullets. I took my best gun, and placed, as usual, my two revolvers in the belt fastened round my waist, then painted my hands and face with powdered charcoal, mixed with palm oil, so that I might appear black. I took Querlaouen with me, telling him that I must kill that gorilla. Querlaouen, at first, did not want to go, "for," said he, "we will never be able to kill that man gorilla." But Querlaouen always obeyed me.

GAMBO'S FRIEND KILLED BY A GORILLA.

We proceeded at once into the thick of the jungle, making for the spot where the poor man had been mortally wounded. I felt very sorry when I saw the place where the man had been killed. A flush came over my face. "Thou shalt be avenged!" I muttered. I looked at my gun with ferocious joy; I held it up, and fondled it, and I must have looked fierce, for poor Querlaouen appeared terrified. "Yes," said I to Querlaouen, "I shall kill that very gorilla."

I followed for a while the tracks of the beast by the marks of blood he had left on the trunks of the trees, but these became less and less noticeable as I removed from the scene of that sad catastrophe. Finally I lost those bloody hand-prints; but then I followed closely, and with great care, other marks he had left in the jungle as he went along. At times I would entirely lose these signs of the huge monster, then I would find them again. I lost them finally, and I searched and searched, but they were not to be seen. I had evidently gone astray. I was so annoyed, so disheartened; for I had set my heart on killing that gorilla, and I was on the point of giving up the chase. Querlaouen kept a few hundred yards from me, and he could see no traces of the gorilla.

Suddenly, and by sheer carelessness, I had stepped on a dead branch of a tree, and broke it. Of course, the breaking of that dry limb made a noise. Immediately I heard a tremendous rush in the jungle, and then saw an intensely black face peering through the leaves. The deep, gray, sunken eyes of the great beast seemed to emit fire when they got sight of me. Then he scattered the jungle with his two hands, raised himself (for he was on all-fours) on his hind legs, gave from that huge chest one of his deep, terrific roars, which shook the whole adjacent forest, and rushed toward me, showing his immense teeth as he opened his mouth.

I had never before seen a gorilla come so quickly to the attack as did this one. He walked in a waddling manner, his two arms extended toward me, his body bent in the same direction, and it seemed to me that at any moment I might see him tumble down on his face. This feeling was caused by his peculiar walk.

I was calm, but it was the calm that precedes death —the feeling that in one minute more I might be a dead man. I am sure not a muscle moved in my face. I was steady, and said to myself, " Paul B. Du Chaillu, you will never go home if you do not kill that creature on the spot, and before he has a chance to get hold of your poor body."

As he approached nearer and nearer, I know that I was cool and determined, but felt that within a few seconds all might be over with me; for, if the diabolical creature once had me in his grasp, he would crush me to death.

Here he is, only five yards distant, but the jungle is so thick that if I fire my bullet may strike the limb of a tree. I wait. I feel that I am as pale as death. I have raised my gun to my shoulder, and follow the movements of the beast, all the time with it pointed at his head. Now he is only four yards distant; I mean his body, for his arms are extended toward me, and are much nearer.

I wait a little longer. He has made one step more toward me; he is within three yards and a half of me. In three or four seconds more he will be a dead gorilla or

I a dead man. Just as he opened his mouth to utter another of his frightful roars, and I could feel his breath on my face, I fired, and shot him right through the heart.

He gave a leap, and fell, with a fearful groan, quite dead, his long, powerful arm almost reaching me as he lay extended on the ground, as if ready to clutch me; but it fell short by a few inches. I drew a heavy breath, for my respiration had become short through excitement. I had a narrow escape, for if the gorilla's hands in falling had reached me they would have lacerated me terribly.

Querlaouen was perfectly wild. While the gorilla was coming to the attack, he cried out with his powerful voice several times, and with all his might, "Kombo, come here if you dare! come here!" He gave a tremendous shout as the gorilla fell, advanced toward the dead monster, fired right into his body, and then whirled round toward me. I thought he had become insane, he looked so wild.

When we went up to the gorilla he was quite dead. His eyes were wide open, his lips shut, and his teeth clinched together. When I took hold of his hand a cold shiver ran through me, it was so big. The hand of Goliath, the giant, could not have been any larger.

When we returned to the camp, and told how we had slain the gorilla, there was immense rejoicing. Soon after a number of men went with Querlaouen to fetch the monster, and when it made its appearance in the village the people became intensely excited, and it was all I could do to prevent them from hacking the body to pieces. I am happy to say, however, that I was able to bring this big specimen to New York.

CHAPTER XVI.

FUNERAL OF THE GORILLA'S VICTIM. — A MAN'S HEAD FOR THE ALUMBI. — THE SNAKE AND THE GUINEA-FOWL. — SNAKE KILLED. — VISIT TO THE HOUSE OF THE ALUMBI. — DETERMINE TO VISIT THE SEA-COAST.

Now the people were to bury the man who had been killed by that big gorilla. His kindred arrived to get the body to carry it to his village. Every man had his body and face painted in all sorts of colors. They also wore their fetiches, and looked like so many devils coming out of the woods.

After traveling the whole day we came to a strange village on the top of a hill, at the foot of which there was a beautiful little stream, the water of which never dried during the season when there was no rain.

As soon as we made our appearance the sounds of wailing and weeping filled the air. The body was taken to the house of the deceased, where his widows—for he had three wives—mourned, and wept, and cried so that I felt the greatest sympathy for them.

At sunset silence reigned in the village. All the women had gone into their huts, while the men seated themselves on the ground or on their little stools. But suddenly a great wailing rent the air, and from every hut came lamentations—sounds that were heart-rending. Then they sang songs, praising the departed one—songs such as I have described to you young folks in "Stories of the Gorilla Country."

At last, after two days, six stout men, covered with fetiches and painted in the most fantastic manner, came to take the body, to leave it in the woods under some big tree.

As soon as they were ready the tam-tams began to beat, and songs of sorrow were chanted as they disappeared from the village. I followed the body, for I wished to see what they would do. After a while we got into the jungle, and soon came to a spot where the body was left. A fire was lighted by its side, no doubt with the idea of keeping him warm; then some boiled plantains, and a piece of cooked elephant and some smoked fish, were put in a dish of wicker-work and placed at his head. All the while the men kept muttering words I did not understand.

The day after the funeral, toward sunset, while I was looking for birds in the forest, trying to obtain some new specimens which I might never have seen before, I fell in with the brother of the deceased, and saw that he was carrying something carefully packed—something which I could not make out. I asked him what it was. At first he replied, "Nothing." Then I said, "You must tell me." Thinking that I was getting angry, he then answered, "Moguizi, I will tell you what it is. It is *the head of my brother* who was buried yesterday, and I have just been to get it." "The head of your brother!" I exclaimed; "and why have you cut off the head of your brother?" "Because," he answered, in a low whisper, "my brother was a great hunter, a mighty warrior, and I want to put his head in the house of the Alumbi. Moguizi, do not tell any one that you have seen me with this head, for we never tell any one when we do this thing, though we all do it. After we have been in the village I will show you the house of the Alumbi."

So I let him go back to his village, and I went hunting for my birds.

As I was returning to my home in the village, I stopped on the bank of the little stream, and there I perceived a very large snake enjoying a bath. As the water was quite clear, I could see him perfectly. I thought I would watch his movements rather than kill him.

The back of this snake was black, and his belly striped yellow and black. It was of a very venomous kind, and one most dreaded by the natives. I could not help a cold shudder running through me as I looked at the reptile. By-and-by it came out of the water and remained still for a little while. Then I saw a beautiful Guinea-fowl coming toward the stream to drink. How beautiful the bird looked! I have before described it in "Stories of the Gorilla Country." He came toward the water, and just as it stood on the brink of the little stream, ready to drink, I saw the huge snake crawling silently toward the bird. It crawled so gently that I could not even hear the noise its body made as it glided over the dead leaves that had fallen from the trees. It came nearer and nearer, and it certainly did not make the noise that it does when not in search of prey.

The poor Guinea-fowl, in the mean time, was unaware of the approach of its enemy, and how greatly its life was in danger. So it lowered its neck and dipped its bill into the water; once, twice, and the snake was getting nearer and nearer; thrice, and the snake was close at hand; and now the snake began to coil itself for a spring. Then the bird took one drink more, and just as it turned its head back its eyes met those of the snake, which stood glaring at the bird. The poor Guinea-fowl stood still, moving not a step, and it was not more than half a yard from the snake, when suddenly the monster sprang with a dart on the poor bird, and before I had time to wink, part of its shiny black body was round the fowl.

How pitiful were the cries of the poor Guinea-fowl! Quick, quick, quick, and all was over. The snake's mouth distended, for he had begun to swallow the bird by the head. Just then I fired in such a way as not to hit the snake, and in his fright he disgorged the bird and left him and the field, crawling out of the way as quick as possible. This time I could hear the noise of the leaves. Indeed, it went off very fast, and I was just on the point of losing sight of it, when I managed to send a load of shot into its body, breaking the spine, as it was about half way across the stream. Then I took a look at the dead Guinea-fowl. Toward the neck the feathers were very slimy from the snake-froth. The snake was now twisting about in all directions, but could neither advance nor retreat, for you know that, its spine being cut, it could not swim, and therefore soon died.

I picked up my Guinea-fowl, cut off the head of the snake, made a parcel of its body, and took the trophies of my day's sport into the village, where I gave a treat to some of my friends.

Soon after my return I went to see my friend Oyagui, who told me in a most mysterious way to wait, and that he would show me the house of the *Alumbi* on the next day.

The next morning I did not see Oyagui, but toward sunset he came with the same mysterious air, and told me to come with him. Then he led me to the rear of his hut, where there was a little dwarfish house, which we entered. There I saw three skulls of men resting on the ochre with which he rubbed his body. One cake was red, another yellow, and another white. There lay the skull of his father, of an uncle, and of a brother. As for the fresh head he had cut the day before, it was not to be seen. There were several fetiches hung above the skulls—fetiches which were famous, and had led his ancestors to victory, gave them success in the hunt, and had prevented them from being bewitched. One of these fetiches had two claws of the eagle called *guanionien*, and three scales of an animal called *ipi*, an ant-eater, the scales on which are very large and thick. This ipi I had thus far never been able to see, though I had heard of it. In the hut was also a plain iron chain, and in the foreground the remains of a burning fire. Oyagui never spoke a word, and after looking round I left, and he closed the door, which was made of the bark of trees.

The people of the village were comparatively strange, and regarded me with some fear. That day there was a new moon. In the evening all was silent; hardly a whisper could be heard. The men had painted their bodies, and there was no dancing or singing, so I retired to my hut, and was soon soundly sleeping.

By this time I began to feel tired of my hard and exciting life, and thought of gradually returning toward the sea-coast. In the morning I had made up my mind to leave, and made preparations accordingly, and on the following day I bade these people good-by, and started on my return.

CHAPTER XVII.

AT WASHINGTON ONCE MORE.—DELIGHTS OF THE SEA-SHORE.
—I HAVE BEEN MADE A MAKAGA.—FRIENDS OBJECT TO
MY RETURN INTO THE JUNGLE.—QUENGUEZA TAKEN SICK.
—GIVES A LETTER TO HIS NEPHEW.—TAKING LEAVE.

TIME passed away. In the mean time I had returned to Washington, that beautiful little village I had built near the sea-shore on the banks of the Fernand Vaz River. I brought down the innumerable trophies of my wanderings while "lost in the jungle"—gorillas, chimpanzees, kooloo-kamba, and other animals; also reptiles. The birds could be counted by thousands, the other specimens by hundreds, all of which I carefully stored.

Every day I would cross the tongue of land separating the Fernand Vaz from the sea, and would go and look at the deep water of the ocean. My eyes would try to look far into the distance, in the hope of spying a sail. There was no vessel for me. I was still alone on that deserted coast of the Gulf of Guinea.

I loved to steal away from Washington, and seat myself all alone on the shore, and look at the big, long, rolling billows of the surf as they came dashing along, white with foam; the booming sound they gave in breaking was like music to me. It was so nice to have left that everlasting jungle; to see prairie land and the wide expanse of the Atlantic; to look at the sun as it disappeared, apparently under the water. How grand the spectacle was! I loved to look at the gulls, to hear their shrill cries, for these cries were so unlike those of the birds of the great forest. There was also something very invigorating in that strong sea breeze that came from the south and southwest. Beyond the breakers I could see now and then the fins of some huge sharks searching for their prey; sometimes they would hardly appear to move, at other times they swam very fast.

The time had not yet come for me to return to New York. I must go back again into the great jungle; I must discover new mountains, new rivers, new tribes of people, new beasts, and new birds; I must have more fights with gorillas, more elephant-hunting. I would be so glad to see Querlaouen, Malaouen, and Gambo.

While I was in the interior, the Commi people, in great council, had made me a *makaga*, which title only one man, and he generally the best hunter and bravest, may bear. The office of the makaga is to lead in all desperate frays. He is the avenger of blood. If any one has murdered one of his fellow-villagers, and the murderer's townspeople refuse to give him up (which almost always happens, for they think it a shame to surrender any one who has taken refuge with them), then it is the office of the makaga to take the great warriors of the tribe, to attack and destroy the village, and cut off the heads of as many people as he can.

If any one is suspected of being a wizard, and runs away from his village, it is the business of the makaga to follow and capture him. In that case he is a kind of sheriff. In fact, he has to see that the laws are executed.

It was only among the Commi that I heard of a makaga.

So you may conceive I did not care to be a makaga, and in a great meeting of the chiefs I declared I could not be. But they all shouted, "We want you, the great slayer of beasts, to be our makaga; we want you to stay with us all the time."

I was getting well and strong again, for I had taken a long rest. I concluded I must go again into the jungle.

My good friend Ranpano said, "Why do you wish to go back into the forest? If you go again to countries where not one black man has ever gone before, we shall never see you again. I have heard that the people want you; they only desire to kill you, for they want to get your skull; they want to make a fetich of your hair. They have many fetiches, but they want one from your hair and brain. We love you; you are our white man. What you tell us to do, we do. When you say it is wrong, we do not do it. We take care of your house, your goats, your fowls, your parrots, your monkeys, and your antelopes;" then shouted with a loud voice, "We love you!"

To which all the people answered, "Yes, we love him. He is our white man, and we have no other white man."

Then the king continued: "We know that writing talks; write to us, therefore, a letter to prove to your friends, if you do not come back, that we have not hurt you; so that when a vessel from the white-man country comes, we can show your letter to the white men." These poor people had an idea that every white man must know me like they knew me.

Finally, when they saw I was bound to go once more

to the jungle, they gave me up, all exclaiming in accents of wonder, "Ottangani angani (man of the white men), what is the matter with you that you have no fear? God gave you the heart of a leopard; you were born without fear!"

Just as I was making the final preparations for my departure, a great trial came upon me. Quengueza, who had accompanied me to the coast, became dangerously ill. There were murmurs among the up-river people.

I began to despair of his life. All the medicine I gave him seemed for a while to do him no good, and he became thinner and thinner every day, till at last he looked almost like a skeleton.

How anxious I felt! Was my great and beloved African friend to die? What would the people say? for I had brought him down from his country. They would surely say that I had killed their king. I could not make out what would be the end if so great a misfortune was to happen. The murmurs of the people, which had already began, caused me sad forebodings of the future.

But there was still a bright spot.

Quengueza knew that, even if I could, I would not make him ill; he knew I loved him too well, and every day he would declare that whoever said that I had made him ill was a liar. And one morning I heard him protest that the man who would say that his friend Chally had made him ill was a wizard. Of course, after such talk, the people took good care to keep their tongues quiet.

Finally he got better and better, and became stronger. What a load of anxiety was removed from my mind!

I felt that I must go now; the rainy season was com-

G

ing on. Quengueza was not strong enough; besides, he wanted to remain, for he had business to transact with some of the sea-shore chiefs after he was well enough to go about.

So Quengueza called one of his nephews of the name of Rapero, and as these people do not write, he gave him "his mouth;" that is to say, he sent word to his brother, or, as I discovered after, to his nephew, who reigned in his stead in Goumbi, to give me as many people as I wanted; and he ordered that his nephew Adouma must be the chief of the party who were to accompany me in the Ashira country, and to take me to Olenda, the king of that people.

My dear little Commi boy Macondai was to come with me, and he was the only one at the sea-side Quengueza would allow to return.

Then, when all was ready for our departure, I went to bid good-by to my two best friends in Africa, King Ranpano and King Quengueza. I have told you before how much I loved King Quengueza, the great chief of the Rembo River. In the presence of all the people, having his idol by his side, covered with the chalk of the Alumbi, he took my two hands in his, the palms of our hands touching each other. Then he invoked the spirits of his ancestor Kombé Ricati Ratenou, and of his mother Niavi, marking me on the forehead with the *mpeshou* (ochre) of his mother Niavi; then he invoked her spirit, for his sake, to protect me, his great friend. He invoked, also, the spirits of his ancestors who had done great deeds to follow me once more in the jungle where he and his people had never been, so that no one could hurt me.

There was a dead silence when the old chief spoke.

BIDDING GOOD-BY TO QUENGUEZA.

After pausing a while, he took a piece of wild cane, which he chewed; then put in his mouth a little piece of the *mpeshou*, and chewed the two together. He then spat the stuff he had chewed on me and round me, still holding my hands, upon which he breathed gently and said, "May the spirits of my ancestors, as the wind that I have blown upon you, follow you wherever you go." And then he shouted with a tremendous voice, "Niavi, Kombé Ricati Ratenou, be with my white man in the jungle where he goes!"

CHAPTER XVIII.

DEPARTURE.—ARRIVAL AT GOUMBI.—THE PEOPLE ASK FOR THE KING.—A DEATH PANIC IN GOUMBI.—A DOCTOR SENT FOR.—DEATH TO THE ANIEMBAS.—THREE WOMEN ACCUSED.—THEY ARE TRIED AND KILLED.

After receiving Quengueza's blessing I jumped in our canoe, and soon the merry sound of the paddles was heard, and once more I ascended the river. The breeze was fresh, the tide was coming in, and every thing was in our favor.

The sickness of Quengueza had delayed me so much that it was now October. We were in the middle of the rainy season, and it was not very comfortable weather for traveling.

My outfit was composed chiefly of powder, shot, bullets, beads, looking-glasses, bracelets of brass and copper, and a lot of trinkets for presents, and also some fine pieces of prints and silks, with a few shirts and coats, for the chiefs. I had also a clock and a musical box.

When we reached Goumbi, the head village of Quengueza's dominions, we were pretty well tired out, for on our way we had encountered two very heavy rain-storms, preceded each by a tornado. The people, not seeing him with me, asked after their king, Quengueza, crying out, "Our king went with you, why have you not brought him back? When he went with you he was well, why has he been sick?"

Then one of the king's nephews gave me Quengueza's house, and Mombou, his head slave, came to receive my orders. Old friend Etia came also, and I was delighted to see him.

Toward sunset I heard a good deal of drumming, and songs being sung to Abambou and Mbuiri. I knew at once by these songs that somebody was very sick. It proved to be Mpomo, one of the nephews of the king. Mpomo was a great friend of mine; his wives and his people had always given me plenty of food, and if you have not heard of him before, it is because he was neither a hunter, a man of the jungle, nor a warrior.

I was asked to go and see him. The people had spent the night before drumming by the side of the bed where he lay, to drive the Abambou and the aniemba away; that is to say, the devil and witchcraft. On entering the hut, I was shocked at the appearance of my old friend. I could see, by his dim eyes, that ne was soon to die, and as I took hold of his wrist and touched his pulse, I found it so weak that I was afraid he could scarcely live through the approaching night. As he saw me, he extended his hands toward me (for I had taught these people to shake hands), and said, in such a pitiful and low voice, "Chally, save me, for I am dying!"

In his hut and outside of it were hundreds of people, most of them moved to tears, for they were afraid that their friend, one of the leading men of the tribe, and one of the nephews of their king, was going to die. His wives were by his bedside, and watched him intently.

I said to him, "Mpomo, I am not God; I am unable to make a tree turn into a fish or an animal. I am a man, and my life is in the hands of God, as yours is.

You must ask God, and not your fetiches, to make you well." Unfortunately, they all thought I could make him well. His friends insisted that I should give him medicine. At last I gave him some. In that country I was afraid to give medicine to men who were very sick. This will seem strange to you, but you will not wonder at it when I tell you that these savages are very superstitious. If the sick person got well after I had given him the medicine, it was all right; but if he got worse, then I was blamed, for they said, "If he had not taken the medicine of the white man instead of our own, he would have got well."

I warned them that I thought Mpomo could not get well. I loved him as well as they did, and felt very sorry. But they all replied, with one voice, "Mpomo will not die unless somebody has bewitched him."

Early the next morning, just before daybreak, the wailings and mournful songs of the natives rent the air. The whole village was in lamentation. Poor Mpomo had just died; he had gone to his long rest. He had died a poor heathen, believing in idols, witchcraft, fetiches, and in evil and good spirits.

How mournful were their cries! "All is done with Mpomo! We shall never see him again! He will never speak to us any more! We shall not see him paddle his canoe any more! He will walk no more in the village!"

At the last moment, when a Commi man is dying, his head wife comes and throws herself beside him on his bed, and surrounds his body with her arms, telling him that she loves him, and begging him not to die. As if the poor man wanted to die!

I immediately went to Mpomo's hut. I saw his poor

wives in tears sitting upon the ground, throwing moistened ashes and dust over their bodies, shaving their hair, and tearing the clothes they wore into rags. Now and then they took the lifeless body of poor Mpomo in their arms; at other times they would kneel at his motionless feet, and implore him to open his eyes and look at them.

As soon as the news of Mpomo's death spread in the village, there was great excitement from one end of it to the other. Fear was on every face; each man and woman thought death was soon to overtake them. Each one dreaded his neighbor; fathers dreaded their sons and their wives; the sons their fathers and mothers; brothers and sisters were in fear of each other. A panic of the wildest kind had spread among the people of Goumbi; neither men nor women were in their senses. They fancied themselves surrounded by the shadow of death, and they saw it ready to get hold of them and carry them away to that last sleep of which they were so afraid.

The people talked of nothing but witchcraft, of wizards, and witches. They were sure that Mpomo had been bewitched.

Two days elapsed before Mpomo was buried, and then a large canoe came, and Mpomo's relatives took the body down the river, where the cemetery of the Abouya clan was situated. This cemetery was some fifty miles down the river, beyond Quayombi.

As the body was placed in the canoe, the people of the whole village mourned. The shrieks of his wives were heart-rending, and it was, who should show the greatest sorrow among the people; for every one was afraid of being accused of aniemba (sorcery); for if they did not appear very sorry, they would be sure to be suspected of being aniembas (sorcerers).

Immediately after the departure of the funeral procession, every man came out armed to the teeth, their faces betokening angry fear, all shouting and screaming, "There are people among us who kill other people. Let us find them out. Let us kill them. How is it—Mpomo was well a few days ago, and now Mpomo is dead?" A canoe was then immediately dispatched among the Bakalai in order to get a celebrated doctor, who had the reputation of being able to discover wizards at once.

The excitement of the savages became extreme. They wanted blood. They wanted to find victims. They wanted to kill somebody. Old and young, men and women, were frantic with a desire for revenge on the sorcerers.

The doctor came. The people surrounded him, shouting, "We have wizards among us. We have sent for you to find them. Do find them out, for if you do not, our people will be dying all the time."

Then the mboundou was prepared. I have described it to you before, and how it is prepared. The doctor drank a big cup of it in one draught.

Oh how his body trembled; how his eyes afterward became bloodshot, his veins enlarged. How the people looked at him with bloodthirsty eyes, and with mouths wide open.

Every man and boy was armed, some with spears, some with swords, some with guns loaded to the muzzle, some with axes and huge knives, and on every face I could see a determination to wreak a bloody revenge on those who should be pointed out as the criminals. The whole people were possessed with an indescribable fury and horrid thirst for human blood.

I shall never forget the sight. There I stood, alone in the midst of this infuriated populace, looking at those faces, so frightened, but, at the same time, so thirsty for blood. A cold shudder ran through me, for I knew not what would come next. I knew not but the whole village of Goumbi might be deluged in blood. I am sure you would have felt as I did.

For the first time my voice was without authority in Goumbi. No one wanted to hear me when I said that nobody must be killed; that there were no such things as sorcerers. "Chally, we are not the same people you are. Our country is full of witchcraft. Death to the wizards!" shouted they all, in tones which made the village shake. "Death to the *aniembas!*"

They were all surrounding the doctor, as I have said before, when, at a motion from the stranger, the people became at once very still. Not a whisper could be heard. How oppressed I felt as I looked on. This sudden silence lasted about one minute, when the loud, harsh voice of the doctor was heard.

The people did not seem to be able to breathe, for no one knew if his name would be the one that should be called, and he be accused of the crime of witchcraft.

"There is a very black woman—a young woman—who lives in a house having one door only, with a large bunch of lilies growing by the door. Not far off is a tree to which the *ogouloungou* birds come every day."

Scarcely had he ended when the crowd, roaring and screaming like so many beasts, rushed frantically for the place indicated, when, to my horror, I saw them enter the hut of my good friend Okandaga, and seize the poor girl, who looked so frightened that I thought she had lost her reason. I shouted with all the power of my voice, "You are not going to kill the beautiful and good Okandaga—the pride and beauty of the village? No," said I, "you are not to kill her." But my voice was drowned. They dragged her from her hut, and waved their deadly weapons over her head. They tore her off, shouting and cursing, and as the poor, good African girl passed in the hands of her murderers, I thought the big tree behind which I was looking might hide me from her view. But lo! she saw me, and with a terrible shriek she cried, extending her arms toward me, "Chally, Chally, do not let me die. Do not let these people kill me. I am not a witch. I have not killed Mpomo. Chally, be a friend to me. You know how I have taken care of you—how I have given you food; how often I have given you water."

I trembled all over. I shook like a reed. It was a moment of terrible agony to me. The blood rushed toward my head. I seized my gun and one of my revolvers which was in my belt. I had a mind to fire into the crowd—shoot people right and left—send dismay among them—rescue dear and kind Okandaga, who was now poor and helpless—who had not a friend; put her in a canoe, and carry her down the river. But then, run away—where? I too would have murdered people. Perhaps some of the nephews of my friend Quengueza would be among those I should kill. Then what should I say to Quengueza? They were too frantic and crazed. The end would have been, I should have been murdered without saving the life of Okandaga. How I cried

"CHALLY, CHALLY, DO NOT LET ME DIE."

that same evening. I remember it so well. I cried like a child. I would have given all I had to save Okandaga's life.

"After all," said I to myself, "what am I?"

They took her toward the banks of the Rembo and bound her with cords.

Quengueza, as you know, was not in Goumbi. How much I wished he had been.

Presently silence fell again upon the crowd. Then the harsh and demon-like voice of the doctor once more rang over the town. It seemed to me like the hoarse croak of some death-foretelling raven.

"There is an old woman not far from the king's place. She lives in a long and narrow house, and just in front of the house are plantain-trees which come from the sprouts which were planted by Oganda, the king's eldest brother, who is now dead. There is also, back of her house, a lime-tree which is now covered with fruit. She has bewitched Mpomo."

Again the crowd rushed off. This time they seized a princess, a niece of King Quengueza, a noble-hearted and rather majestic old woman. As they crowded about her with flaming eyes and threats of death, she rose proudly from the ground, looked them in the face unflinchingly, and, motioning them to keep their hands off her, said, "I will drink the mboundou, for I am not a witch; and woe to my accusers if I do not die!"

The crowd shouted and vociferated. Then she too was escorted to the river, but was not bound. She submitted to all without a tear or a murmur for mercy; she was too proud. Belonging directly to the families of the chiefs of the Abonya tribes from times of which they had no record, she wanted to show that she was not afraid of death. Pride was in her features, and she looked haughtily at her accusers, who left a strong guard, and then went back to the doctor.

Again, a third time, the dreadful silence fell upon the town, and the doctor's voice was heard.

Oh how I hated that voice!

"There is a woman with six children—she lives on a plantation toward the rising sun — she too bewitched Mpomo."

Again there was a furious shout, and the whole town seemed to shake under the uproar of voices clamoring for vengeance. A large squad of people rushed toward a plantation not far from the village. They returned soon after, appearing frantic, as if they were all crazy, and went toward the bank of the river, dragging with them one of King Quengueza's slaves, a good woman who many and many a time had brought me baskets of ground-nuts, bunches of bananas, and plantains. Her they took to where the two others were.

Then the doctor descended the street of the village. How fierce he looked! He wore round his waist a belt made from the skin of a leopard; on his neck he wore the horn of an antelope, filled with charmed powder, and hanging from it was a little bell. Round his belt hung long feathers of the ogouloungou bird; on his wrists he wore bracelets made from the bones of snakes; while round his neck were several cords, to which were attached skins of wild animals, tails of monkeys, leopards' and monkeys' teeth, scales of pangolins, and curious-looking dry leaves mingled with land and river shells. His face was painted red, his eyebrows white, and all over his body were scattered white and yellow spots. His teeth were filed to a point, and altogether he looked horrid. I wish I could have shot that monster; but then they all think alike—they all believe in witchcraft. He approached the women, and the crowd surrounded them.

Silence again succeeded to that great uproar; the wind seemed to whisper through the boughs of the trees; the tranquil river glided down, whose waters were soon to be stained with blood.

In a loud voice the doctor recited the crime of which the three women were accused. Then, pointing to Okandaga, he said that she had, a few weeks before, asked Mpomo for some salt, he being her relative. "Salt was scarce," said he, looking toward the frantic multitude, "and Mpomo refused her; she said unpleasant words to him, for she was angry that he had refused her salt. Then she vowed to bewitch him, and had succeeded, and by sorcery had taken his life."

The people shouted, "Oh, Okandaga, that is the way you do—you kill people because they do not give you what you ask. You shall drink the mboundou! That sweet face of yours is that of a witch. Ah! ah! ah! and we did not know it."

The crime of Quengueza's niece came next to be told. She had been jealous of Mpomo for a long time because he had children and she had none. She envied him; therefore jealousy and envy took possession of her, and she bewitched him.

The people screamed, "How could a woman be so wicked as to kill a man because he had children and she had none! We will give you mboundou to drink, and we will see if you are not a witch."

Quengueza's slave had asked Mpomo for a looking-glass. He had refused her, and therefore she had killed him with sorcery also.

As each accusation was recited the people broke out in curses. Each one rivaled his neighbor in cursing the victims, fearful lest lukewarmness in the ceremony should expose him to a like fate. So Okandaga's father, mother, brother, and sisters joined in the curses. The king's niece was cursed by her brothers and sons, and the poor slave by every body. It was a fearful scene to contemplate.

Then a passage was formed in the vast crowd, and the three women were led to the river, where a large canoe was in waiting. The executioners went in first, then the women, the doctor, and a number of people well armed with huge knives and axes.

By this time the sweat ran down my face. I must have been deadly pale as I followed each motion of these people.

Then the tam-tams beat, and the proper persons prepared the mboundou.

Quabi, Mpomo's eldest brother, who was to inherit all of Mpomo's property, held the poisoned cup. At sight of it poor Okandaga began again to cry, and Quengueza's niece turned pale in the face, for even the negro face at such times attains a pallor which is quite perceptible. Three other canoes, full of armed men, surrounded that in which the victims were.

A mug full of mboundou was then handed to the old slave woman, next to the royal niece, and last to the young and kind Okandaga. As they drank, the multitude shouted, "If they are witches, let the mboundou kill them; if they are innocent, let the mboundou go out!"

It was the most exciting scene in my life. My arrival in the cannibal country was as nothing compared with this. Though horror froze my blood, my eyes were riveted upon the spectacle. I could not help it. Suddenly the slave fell down. She had not touched the boat's bottom before her head was hacked off by a dozen rude swords, the people shouting "Kill her! kill her!" Next came Quengueza's niece. In an instant her head was off, and her blood was dyeing the waters of the river.

During all this time my eyes had been riveted on poor Okandaga. I hoped that she would not fall, but soon she too staggered, and struggled, and cried, vainly resisting the effects of the poison in her system. There was a dead silence—the executioners themselves were still—for Okandaga was the belle of the village, and had more lovers than any body else; but, alas! she finally fell, and in an instant her head was hewn off.

Then all was confusion. In an incredibly short space of time the bodies were cut in pieces and thrown in the river.

I became dizzy; my eyes wandered about; the perspiration fell down from my face in big drops; I could hardly breathe, and I thought I would fall insensible. One scene more like this, and I should have become mad. The image of poor Okandaga was before me, begging me to save her. I retired to my hut, but it felt so hot inside that I could not stay.

When all was over, the crowd dispersed without saying a word; the clamor ceased, and for the rest of the day the village was silent.

In the evening my friend Adouma, uncle of Okandaga, came secretly to my house to tell me how sorry he was that Okandaga had been killed. He said, "Chailly, I was compelled to take part in the dreadful scene. I was obliged to curse Okandaga, but what my mouth said my heart denied. If I had acted otherwise I should have been a dead man before now."

I then spoke to Adouma of the true God, and told him that nothing in the world lasted forever. Men, women, and children died, just as he saw young and old trees die. Often a young tree would die before an old one. Hence young men and young women would frequently die before older ones.

CHAPTER XIX.

QUENGUEZA ORDERS ILOGO TO BE CONSULTED ABOUT HIS ILLNESS.—WHAT THE PEOPLE THINK OF ILOGO.—A NOCTURNAL SÉANCE.—SONG TO ILOGO.—A FEMALE MEDIUM.—WHAT ILOGO SAID.

WHAT a strange village Goumbi is! It is well that I am the friend of King Quengueza. The people are so superstitious. We had hardly got over the affair of witchcraft when the people declared they must find some means of ascertaining the cause of the king's sufferings. Quengueza had sent word himself that his people must try to find out from *Ilogo* why he was sick, and what he must do for his recovery.

Ilogo is believed by the people to be a spirit living in the moon—a mighty spirit, who looks down upon the inhabitants of the earth—a spirit to whom the black man can talk. "Yes," they said, "Ilogo's face can be seen; look at it." Then they pointed out to me the spots on the moon which we can see with our naked eye. These spots were the indistinct features of the spirit.

One fine evening, at full moon (for, to consult Ilogo, the moon must be full, or nearly so), the women of the village assembled in front of the king's house. Clustered close together, and seated on the ground, with their faces turned toward the moon, they sang songs. They were surrounded by the men of the village. I shall not soon forget that wild scene. The sky was clear and beautiful; the moon shone in its brightness, eclipsing by its light that of the stars, except those of the first magnitude; the air was calm and serene, and the shadows of the tall trees upon the earth appeared like queer phantoms.

THE SONGS TO ILOGO.

The songs of the women were to and in praise of Ilogo, the spirit that lived in ogouayli (the moon). Presently a woman seated herself in the centre of the circle of singers and began a solo, gazing steadfastly at the moon, the people every now and then singing in chorus with her. She was to be inspired by the spirit Ilogo to utter prophecies.

At last she gave up singing, for she could not get into a trance. Then another woman took her place, in the midst of the most vociferous singing that could be done by human lips. After a while the second woman gave place to a third—a little woman, wiry and nervous. She seated herself like the others, and looked steadily at the moon, crying out that she could see Ilogo, and then the singing redoubled in fury. The excitement of the people had at that time become very great; the drums beat furiously, the drummers using all their strength, until covered with perspiration; the outsiders shouted madly, and seemed to be almost out of their senses, for their faces were wrinkled in nervous excitement, their eyes perfectly wild, and the contortions they made with their bodies indescribable.

The excitement was now intense, and the noise horrible. The songs to Ilogo were not for a moment discontinued, but the pitch of their voices was so great and so hoarse that the words at last seemed to come with difficulty. The medium, the women, and the men all sang with one accord:

"Ilogo, we ask thee,
Tell who has bewitched the king!
Ilogo, we ask thee,
What shall we do to cure the king?
The forests are thine, Ilogo!
The rivers are thine, Ilogo!
The moon is thine!
O moon! O moon! O moon!
Thou art the home of Ilogo!
Shall the king die? O Ilogo!
O Ilogo! O moon! O moon!"

These words were repeated over and over, the people getting more terribly excited as they went on. The woman who was the medium, and who had been singing violently, looked toward the moon, and began to tremble. Her nerves twitched, her face was contorted, her muscles swelled, and at last her limbs straightened out. At this time the wildest of all wild excitement possessed the people. I myself looked on with intense curiosity. She fell on her back on the ground, insensible, her face turned up to the moon. She looked as if she had died in a fit.

The song to Ilogo continued with more noise than ever; but at last comparative quiet followed, compelled, I believe, by sheer exhaustion from excitement. But the people were all gazing intently on the woman's face.

I shall not forget that scene by moonlight, nor the corpse-like face of that woman, so still and calm. How wild it all looked! The woman, who lay apparently dead before the savages, was expected at this time to see things in the world of Ilogo—that is to say, the moon—to see the great spirit Ilogo himself; and, as she lay insensible, she was supposed to be holding intercourse with him. Then, after she had conversed with the great spirit Ilogo, she would awake, and tell the people all she saw and all that Ilogo had said to her.

For my part, I thought she really was dead. I approached her, and touched her pulse. It was weak, but there was life. After about half an hour of insensibility she came to her senses, but she was much prostrated. She seated herself without rising, looking round as if stupefied. She remained quite silent for a while, and then began to speak.

"I have seen Ilogo, I have spoken to Ilogo. Ilogo has told me that Quengueza, our king, shall not die; that Quengueza is going to live a long time; that Quengueza was not be... that a remedy prepared from such a p... (the name) would cure him. Then," she ... ut to sleep, and when I awoke Ilogo was ... I find myself in the midst of you."

...ople then quietly separated, as by that time ...late, and all retired to their huts, I myself going ...mine, thinking of the wild scene I had just witnessed, and feeling that, the longer I remained in that strange country, the more strange the customs of the people appeared to me. Soon all became silent, and nothing but the barking of the watchful little native dogs broke the stillness of the night. The moon continued to shine over that village, the inhabitants of which had run so wild with superstition.

CHAPTER XX.

DEPARTURE FROM GOUMBI.—QUERLAOUEN'S VILLAGE.—FIND IT DESERTED.—QUERLAOUEN DEAD.—HE HAS BEEN KILLED BY AN ELEPHANT.—ARRIVE AT OBINDJI'S TOWN.—MEETING WITH QUERLAOUEN'S WIDOW.—NEITHER MALAOUEN NOR GAMBO AT HOME.

AFTER a few days thus spent in Goumbi, we had to get ready to be off.

Adouma made the preparations for our journey; canoes were lying on the banks of the river, waiting to carry the people Quengueza had ordered to go with me. These were, for the most part, the king's slaves. Plantains and cassava had been gathered for our journey. We were to ascend the river as far as Obindji.

One fine morning we started, several very large canoes being filled with men who were to escort me.

Adouma was in my canoe, holding a large paddle as a rudder. We were in a canoe which was chiefly loaded with my outfit and presents.

We left Goumbi silently, for the death of Mpomo made singing out of order. The people were in mourning.

Some of the men who were to accompany me had most curious names, such as Gooloo-Gani, Biembia, Agambie-Mo, Jombai, Monda, Akondogo.

The day became exceedingly hot and sultry, and toward evening we were overtaken by a terrible storm of wind and rain—a real tornado burst upon us.

The next morning we were on our way for the upper river.

I was glad I was about to see my old friend Querlaouen once more. I was also to see my other friends, Malaouen and Gambo.

I had nice presents for Querlaouen, and pretty beads for his wife and children. Among the presents for Querlaouen was a handsome gun and a keg of powder for shooting elephants, leopards, gorilla, and all sorts of wild game.

As we ascended the river I recognized the point on the other side of which was Querlaouen's plantation. I ordered the men to sing, in order that Querlaouen might thus hear of our arrival. The nearer we came to the point the louder became the beatings of my heart. To see old Querlaouen, with whom I had had so many pleasant days; who had bravely shared all kinds of danger with me, including hunger and starvation; with whom I had slain gorilla—I was in a hurry to give to him and his wife their presents. To see such a friend was indeed to have a great treat.

Our canoes soon passed the point. I was looking eagerly, watching for somebody on the river bank. No one! Perhaps our songs had not pierced through the woods. The wind was coming from an opposite direction.

"Sing louder," I exclaimed, for I fancied they did not sing loud enough. They looked at me as if they would have said, "What's the matter with Chally, he looks so excited?" Little did they know my feelings, and how my heart beat for Querlaouen.

They sang louder, till I could hear the echo of their voices among the hills that surrounded us. I looked, but no one was on the shore. Querlaouen might have gone hunting, but surely his wife, or brother, or some of his children must be there. All was silent.

I shouted with all my power, "Querlaouen, your friend Chally has come! your friend Chally has come!" but the hills sent back the echo of my voice to me. I fired a gun, and the echo resounded from hill to hill, and no one came. I began to feel oppressed. A presentiment flashed over my mind. Was Querlaouen dead?

At last I landed on the very shore where Querlaouen lived. Again I shouted, "Querlaouen, where are you?" I called his wife. The silence of death was there.

I advanced, but lo! when I reached the village, it was deserted. Not a soul was seen. The jungle was the thickest where his little clearing had been. The houses had tumbled down. Desolation was before me. The grass had grown to a man's height in the little street.

What a pang of sorrow shot through my heart! I could not help it. I shouted, "Querlaouen! my friend Querlaouen, what has become of you? You are not dead, are you?" and I looked with profound sadness on the scene around. Days that had passed came to my memory.

I retraced my steps, disappointed, and with a foreboding heart. On the river bank, just as I was on the point of stepping into the canoe, a Bakalai came out from the jungle. He had recognized me, and came to meet me.

As soon as I saw him, I cried out, "Where is friend Querlaouen?" His answer seemed so long in coming— "Dead!"

"Dead!" I exclaimed; "Querlaouen dead!" and, I could not help it, two tears rolled down my cheeks.

"Querlaouen dead!" I repeated again. The recollection of that good and noble savage flashed upon me as fast as thought can flash, and once more and in a low voice I said, "Dead! Querlaouen dead!"

When I became composed again, I asked, "How did he die?"

"One day," said the Bakalai man, "a few *moons* ago—it was in the dry season—Querlaouen took his gun and a slave along with him, and went out into the woods to hunt after an elephant which had the day before destroyed a whole plantation of plantain-trees, and had trampled down almost a whole patch of sugar-cane. His slave, who accompanied him, but had left him for a few minutes to look at one of the plantations close by, heard the report of Querlaouen's gun. He waited for his return, but Querlaouen did not come back. He waited so long that he began to feel anxious, and at last set out to seek him. He found him in the forest dead, and trampled into a shapeless mass by the beast, which he had wounded mortally, but which had strength enough to rush at and kill its enemy. Not far from Querlaouen lay the elephant, dead."

How poor Querlaouen, who was so prudent a hunter, could have been caught by the elephant, I could not learn.

The man said it was an aniemba (witchcraft) that had killed Querlaouen; that Querlaouen's brother had bewitched him, and caused, by witchcraft, the elephant to trample upon him.

The brother was killed by the mboundou which the

people made him drink; for they said his brother made him go hunt that day, when he knew the elephant would kill him.

That family, who really loved each other, and lived in peace and unity, was then divided asunder. The brother being killed, the women and children had gone to live with those to whom they belonged by the law of inheritance, and were thus scattered in several villages.

With a heavy heart I entered my canoe, but not before giving a bunch of beads to the Bakalai who had told me the story of the untimely death of poor Querlaouen.

We ascended the river silently, I thinking of the frailty of human life, and that perhaps a day might come when some elephant would trample upon me, or some ferocious leopard carry me away in his jaws, or some gorilla would, with one blow of his powerful hand, cut my body in two. Perhaps fever might kill me. I might encounter an unfriendly tribe and be murdered.

I raised a silent prayer to the Great Ruler of the universe to protect me, and said, "God, thou knowest that I am guided only by the love of discovering the wonders of thy creation, so that I may tell to my fellow-creatures all that I have seen. I am but a worm; there is no strength in me. What am I in this great forest?" Oh how helpless I felt. The news of Querlaouen's death had very much depressed my spirits, casting a heavy gloom over me.

To this day I love to think of friend Querlaouen, of his family, and of his children, and of the great hunts we have had together.

We finally approached Obindji's town, and soon were

landed on the shore, where his little village was built with the bark of trees.

I need not say what a welcome we received. But lo! what do I see? Querlaouen's wife! She had come here on a visit. As is customary in that country for friends who have not seen each other for a long time, we embraced.

The good woman was so glad to see me. She still wore the marks of her widowhood. Her hair was shorn, she wore no ornament whatever, and did not even wash.

She spent the evening with me, telling me all her troubles, and that, as soon as her season of widowhood was finished, she was to become the wife of Querlaouen's youngest brother. "But," added she, "I will never love any one as I loved Querlaouen." She was to live in the mountains of the Ashankolo.

This was probably the last time I was to see the wife of my good friend Querlaouen, the Bakalai hunter, and all the friendship I ever had for her husband was now hers; so I went quietly to one of my chests, and, taking a necklace of large beads, fixed it round her neck; then put my hand on the top of her head, and gave her a *bongo* (a law), which was, that she must never part with these beads, and that, as years would roll by, she must say, "These beads came from Chally, Querlaouen's friend."

The old woman was so much touched that she trembled, and tears stood in her eyes.

After keeping the necklace for two or three minutes round her neck, she took it off, for a woman in mourning can not wear any ornaments. She said she would keep the beads till she died, and then they should be buried with her. I gave her some other presents, which

GIVING BEADS TO QUEBLAOUEN'S WIFE.

she hid, "for," said she, "if the people knew I had such nice things, they might bewitch me in order to obtain them. Chally, the country is full of aniemba." These last words she uttered in a very low voice.

Obindji told me that he had heard Malaouen had gone on some trading expedition. I had, therefore, only to regret not being able to see him or Gambo, who had returned to his own country.

I missed them dreadfully, and I left word with Obindji to tell them to come to the Ashira country after me.

I could not possibly remain, and all the entreaties of friend Obindji could not make me stay. I must go to the Ashira country.

In the mean time, a new comer is to be one of the chiefs of the party. Okendjo, an Ashira man, with Adouma, is going to lead us. Adouma received very positive orders from the king to follow me to the Ashira country. Wherever I go, he must not return without me.

With Bakalai and Goumbi people, amounting to thirty-two men all told, I left the morning after my arrival for the Ashira land.

Okendjo was in his glory; he had conceived the brilliant idea of taking the first moguizi into his country.

CHAPTER XXI.

LEAVE FOR ASHIRA LAND.—IN A SWAMP.—CROSS THE MOUNTAINS. — A LEOPARD AFTER US. — REACH THE ASHIRA COUNTRY.

EARLY on that morning of my departure for the Ashira Land we were awakened by the voice of friend Obindji, who was recommending Okendjo to take great care of his "white man," and see that nothing should hurt him.

We were soon under way, and, leaving the Ovenga, ascended the Ofoubou River for three miles and a half, when we unloaded our canoes. Then we struck off due east.

We had very great trouble in getting through the marshy lands which border the river, for they were overflowed to the very foot of the hills.

This was about as hard a piece of traveling as I ever had in my life. The water was so yellow that I could not see to the bottom, which was slimy clay, covering the roots of trees.

I hardly entered the swamp before down I seated myself in a manner I did not like at all. I barely saved my gun from going to the bottom. My foot had slipped on a root. Then I went tottering along, getting hold of all the branches or trees I could reach, at the same time saying to myself that I did not see the use of such a country.

I was in water from my knees to my waist; below my knees I was in mud. I felt warm enough, for at every step I would go deeper into the sticky mud, and it was difficult to get my feet out again. I took good care to have Okendjo and two or three fellows go ahead of me. They had no clothes, and if they tumbled into the water I did not care; they were not long in drying off.

Finally we got through, and stood at the foot of a mountain ridge along which, we may say, lay the route leading to Ashira Land. Here we gave three cheers, and with cheery hopes I started once more for a *terra incognita*.

We are lost in the jungle. Under the tall trees a dense jungle covers the ground; lianas hang gracefully from the limbs and trunks of trees. Many of them are covered with flowers. Now and then, huge blocks of quartz rocks are met with. We go along slowly, for we are tired.

Okendjo says that soon we shall reach the promised land, where goats, fowls, plantain, and palm wine are plentiful.

Mountain after mountain had to be ascended. Oh, how hard we worked! How we panted after reaching the summit of a hill. How beautiful were the rivulets, they were so pure, so cool, so nice; their crystalline water rolled in every direction, tumbling over the rocks in foaming cascades, or purling along in a bed of white pebbles. Oh how much they reminded me of the hill-streams and trout-brooks of home; for if the trees I saw had not the foliage of our trees at home, the stones were the same. The quartz was similar. Nature there, at least, was alike. The rocks were of the same formation.

I felt well and happy. I was on my way to discover new lands, new rivers, new mountains, and new beasts

GOING TO ASHIRA LAND.

and birds. I was to see new tribes of men whom I had never seen before.

So I trotted along, Okendjo, Adouma, and I leading the way. By-and-by the country became still more rugged. The blocks of quartz we met were of larger size, and soon our path led us in the midst of huge masses of stones. How queer and small we looked as our caravan filed, one by one, between the ponderous blocks! We looked exactly like pigmies alongside of the huge boulders.

Quite near us were some large ebony-trees; how beautiful their foliage looked, contrasting with the blocks of quartz and granite, some of which were covered with mosses, and others perfectly bare. What could have brought these huge boulders on those mountains? I should not wonder if glaciers had accomplished it in ages that are past. The more rocky the soil, the better ebony-trees appeared to flourish.

How hard the walking was! In many places the rains had washed away the soil from the immense and wide-spreading roots, which ran along the ground like huge serpents—indeed, many of them were just like big boa constrictors.

My feet were so sore by walking on those roots, or rather by stepping from one to another, for I was obliged to wear thin-soled shoes, so that I might bend my feet to seize the roots. If I had worn thick shoes I should have tumbled down at the first jump.

Just before sunset we stopped, and I ordered the camp to be built, the firewood to be collected for the night. There were no large leaves to be found, so we all hoped that no rain or tornado would come that night.

We all made beds of such leaves as were to be found; for myself, I put two mats on the top, and lighted, as usual, four fires round me to keep off the wild beasts.

The Bakalai built a camp for themselves, the Ashira built another, and my own was between the two. I lay down, feeling very tired, and prayed to God to take care of me. For a pillow I used the belt which held my revolvers, and taking one of my guns in my arms, I went to sleep.

Toward one o'clock in the morning I was awakened by the loud roaring of a leopard which was prowling round our camp. He had smelled human flesh; probably he had tasted it before, but he dared not approach very close, for the fires were bright and the men awake. He was afraid of the bright light, and his howls testified how enraged he was. He was, no doubt, hungry, but his cowardice kept him back. I ordered some guns to be fired at random in the direction where we heard his growls.

For a while the forest became silent, and the leopard went off. We thought we had frightened him; but, just as we were on the point of going to sleep once more, suddenly the roaring began again, and this time the beast had come nearer. He wanted, no doubt, to make his breakfast upon one of us; but his desires were not to be gratified. I felt mad, as I wanted to sleep, for the next day was to be one of hard traveling.

If I had dared, I would have ventured into the forest after the beast; but the risk was too great, it was so dark. The leopard would have done, no doubt, as cats do, lain flat on the ground and waited for his prey, and pounced upon me as the smaller animal would do upon a mouse. So, as the roars of the beast continued, we concluded to keep awake, first putting more wood on our fires.

The loads we had carried since leaving Obindji had been very heavy, and the sore backs of the men began to show that they had hard work. I was loaded as well as any of them, with powder, shot, my own food, bullets for my gun and my revolvers, which I carried in my belt, an extra pair of pantaloons, shoes, etc., etc.

Resuming our journey next morning, I discovered that the fellows had either been eating lots of plantains, or perhaps slyly throwing away a quantity of them, in order to be relieved of the burden. I warned them that if we were short of food they would have to starve first.

They replied, "There are plenty of nuts in the forest —there are plenty of berries in the forest; we can stand being a day without food!"

Toward the evening of that day we began to see signs of a change in the face of the country. Now and then we would pass immense plantations of plantains, the trees loaded with fruit. We came at last to one which gorillas had visited and made short work of, having demolished lots of trees, which lay scattered right and left. Elephants had also made sad havoc in some of the plantations. Then we came across patches of sugar-cane. These plantations were scattered in the great forest, and grew in the midst of innumerable trunks and dead branches of trees that had been cut down.

The soil became more clayey, and at last we emerged from the immense forest. I saw, spread out before me, a new country, the like of which I had not seen since I had been lost in the great equatorial jungle. It was Ashira Land. The prairies were dotted plentifully with villages, which looked in the distance like ant-hills.

CHAPTER XXII.

GREAT MOUNTAINS.—ASHIRA LAND IS BEAUTIFUL.—THE PEOPLE ARE AFRAID.—REACH AKOONGA'S VILLAGE.—KING OLENDA SENDS MESSENGERS AND PRESENTS.—I REACH OLENDA'S VILLAGE.

WHAT a beautiful country! How lovely the grass seemed to me! How sweet it was to see an open space!

"Where are we?" cried I to my Okendjo men.

They answered, in Ashira Land—Otobi (prairie). It seemed to me that they should have replied in Fairyland, as I had been so long shut up in the dark forest.

I stood for a long time on a bluff just on the border of the forest. On the left, in the far distance, loomed up mountains higher than any I had yet seen. They looked very beautiful against the blue sky. These mountains were called Nkoumou-Nabouali. No one had ever been on their summit. On the right, in the distance also, were mountains, but not so lofty, called Ofoubou-Orèrè and Andelè, and in front of my position were still other mountains called Okoukoué.

All over the prairies villages were scattered, and the hills and valleys were streaked with ribbon-like paths, while here and there my eye caught the silver sheen of a brook winding along through the undulating land. I could also see groves of banana and plantain trees, with their leaves so large and beautiful. There were likewise plantations of cassada and peanuts.

The setting sun shone over the landscape, and the tall green grass reminded me of home, and my heart at once went over the sea. Do not think that I was without feeling because I went to Africa and left civilization—that I never thought of friends. There were girls and boys of whom I thought almost every day, and whom I loved dearly.

"Fire a gun," said Okendjo; "fire, Moguizi, so that my people may know you by the thunder you carry in your hand, and that Okendjo brings them a moguizi."

The good fellow was in a high state of excitement. Adouma was nowhere. I loaded my guns with heavy charges, and fired, bang! bang! bang! Immediately I could see the people running out of their villages; they seemed in the distance like pigmies; they shouted, and were, perhaps, just a little frightened as they ran to and fro. They had seen the smoke and heard the noise, and soon they saw me. Okendjo had sent guides to tell the people not to be afraid; besides, my fame had gone before me, for many of the Ashira had seen me.

We did not long remain motionless, for it was almost dark, and we must hurry. Soon every hill-top was covered with people, but as we passed by they ran away.

Okendjo walked ahead of me, shouting "Ashira! I have brought to you a great and mighty spirit! He is good, and does no harm! Ashira! I am Okendjo."

The crowd shouted in reply, "The ntangani has come! The moguizi has come to see our land—our land which he never saw before. Moguizi, we will give you plenty to eat! Moguizi, do us no harm! Oh, Moguizi!" Then they sung songs, and the idols were brought out, so that they might see the moguizi that had come. The drums beat, but, as I have said, when I came near, the people ran away, leaving their idols behind to look at me.

Indeed, the Ashira Land was a strange country.

We soon came to a village, the chief of which was Okendjo's brother; his name was Akoonga. He was at the gate of the village, and trembled with fear, but he had come to welcome me.

"Am I tipsy with plantain wine? Do tell me, Okendjo, if I see aright, or is it a hallucination of my mind? Have I not before me the spirit who makes the guns, the beads, the brass rods, and the copper rings?

"Do I see aright when I see that his hair is long, and as black as that of the mondi? when I see that his legs are black, and that he has no toes (I had boots on)? that his face is of a color I never saw? Do tell me—tell me quick, Okendjo, am I drunk?"

Okendjo replied, "He is the spirit of whom you have heard so much, who came into the Bakalai country. He comes from the spirit land to visit us." The people then shouted, "How queer the spirit looks!" My hair was long, very long, and excited their wonder.

Akoonga soon gave me a house. There the chief came, followed by ten of his wives, each bearing two bunches of plantains, which, with fear and trembling, they brought to my feet. Then came four goats, twenty fowls, several baskets of ground-nuts, and many bunches of sugar-cane.

The chief told Okendjo to say to me that he was glad I was to spend the night in his village, and that I was the master of every thing in it.

When night came Okendjo walked from one end of the village to the other, and I heard him say to his people, "Be silent; do not trouble the spirit; do not speak, lest you awake him, and he might awake in anger, and smite you, and make the people of our village die. Neither our forefathers nor ourselves ever saw such a wonder as this."

Next morning immense crowds surrounded the village. They shouted and shouted, and, not to disappoint them, I walked through the street from time to time.

Olenda, the king or head chief of the Ashiras, for whose place I was bound, sent presents of goats and plantains for the spirit by two messengers, and wanted to know if the arrival of the moguizi was true. The king also sent word that I should be carried; for why should the moguizi walk if he is tired?

The messengers went and reported to their king that it was so—a good moguizi had come. Then a great number of men were sent back to carry my baggage, and we left Akoonga's village. The men shouted, and from time to time sung wild songs celebrating my arrival among them. After a walk of ten miles I reached the village of Olenda. Olenda was the great king of the Ashira tribe.

CHAPTER XXIII.

KING OLENDA COMES TO RECEIVE ME. — HE IS VERY OLD. — NEVER SAW A MAN SO OLD BEFORE. — HE BEATS HIS KENDO. — HE SALUTES ME WITH HIS KOMBO. — KINGS ALONE CAN WEAR THE KENDO.

OLENDA village was situated at the top of a high hill. The people, with the exception of a few, had fled. All were afraid to see the moguizi close by them.

"How could King Olenda run off, when his great friend Quengueza sent him a moguizi?" shouted Okendjo; "the people will return when they see Olenda facing you."

I was led to the ouandja, and had scarcely seated myself on a native stool when I heard the sound of the kendo—the king was coming. The kendo was ringing, and no one can possess or ring a kendo but a king. So, at every step the king made the kendo rang, and at last Olenda stood before me.

Never in my life had I seen a man so old; never did I dream that a man could be so old, and I wondered not that his fame had spread far and wide on account of his age. He was a man with wool as white as snow, and his face was a mass of wrinkles. Every rib could be seen, for the skin was like parchment. His body was bent almost double with age, and the legs and arms were like sticks, apparently not bigger than broom-handles. His

RECEPTION OF THE KING OF THE ASHIRAS.

cheeks were so hollow that the skin seemed to cling to the bones. He had painted with the chalk of the Alumbi his haggard old face, red on one side and white on the other, in streaks, and, as he stood before me, I wondered as much at his appearance as he did at mine. He carried a long stick or cane to support himself. The like I had never seen. He seemed the apparition of some man who had lived in our world a couple of hundred years.

When we had gazed at each other (he looking at me with deep little eyes for at least five minutes, and beating his kendo all the time with his palsied hand), he suddenly spoke and said, "I have no bowels; I am like the Ovenga River—I can not be cut in two. I am also like the Niembai and Ovenga Rivers, which unite together. Thus my body is united, and nothing can divide it."

This gibberish had some deep mystic significance. It was the regular and invariable salutation of the Ashira kings, Olenda's predecessors, time out of mind. Each chief and important person has such a salutation, which they call *kombo*.

I will explain Olenda's kombo to you. If you had before you a map of the countries I have explored in Equatorial Africa, which are published in my larger works, you would see on it the River Ovenga. Olenda means, when he says that he can not be cut in two and is like the River Ovenga, that his body can not be divided any more than the River Ovenga can be cut in twain. The Niembai and Ovenga unite together and form one river, called Rembo; so, if his body was cut in two, it could not be separated, for, as the two rivers unite and form one, so the two parts of his body would reunite again and form one.

Then he continued, beating his kendo from time to time, "You, the spirit, have come to see Olenda; you, the spirit, have put your feet where none like you have ever been. You are welcome."

Here the old king's son, also a very old negro, with white wool on his head, handed over to the king two slaves, which his majesty formally presented to me, together with three goats, twenty bunches of plantains, twenty fowls, five baskets of ground-nuts, and several bunches of sugar-cane.

"This," said he, "is to salute you. Whatever else you want, tell me. I am the king of this country; I am older than any tree you see around you."

I replied that slaves I did not want, but the food and other presents I would take.

Then more of the old man's children came, all old, and wrinkled, and white-headed men. They stood before me, regarding me with wonder and awe, while the people, of whom thousands were gathered from all the villages of the plain, had returned while their old king was speaking to me. They looked on in silence, and expressed their surprise in whispers.

At last the old king turned to his people and said, "I have seen many things in my life—many wonderful things; but now I am ready to die, for I have received the moguizi spirit, from whom we receive all things. It will always be said in our nation, by those coming after us, that in the time of Olenda the spirit first appeared and dwelt among us. You are welcome (turning to me). Keep this spirit well (to his people); he will do us good."

I was amazed; my eyes could not keep away from Olenda. I knew not that men could become so old.

Then Olenda began to beat his kendo again, invoking the spirits of his ancestors to be with him and his, and, with his body bent double, and supported by his cane, he returned to his hut, ejaculating "*Ma-mo, ma-mo, ma-mo!*"

The kendo is the symbol of royalty in most of the tribes of this part of the interior of Africa. It is a rude bell of iron, furnished with a long handle, also of iron, and of the same piece, as shown in the engraving. The sound, which at home announces the vicinity of a herd of cows or sheep, in Africa precedes the advent of the sovereign, who uses the kendo only when on visits of state or on business of importance. When not beating it they wear it on the shoulder. The bell may vary from six to eight inches in length, and the handle from twelve to fifteen inches. When they wear the kendo they fill it with a skin, generally of an oshengui, which contains monda, or charms, to keep away the aniemba.

A nice little hut was given to me, and I was soon safely housed in it. One of the chickens given to me by Olenda was killed, and a soup made with it. It was excellent, and did me good.

CHAPTER XXIV.

THEY ALL COME TO SEE ME.—THEY SAY I HAVE AN EVIL EYE.—ASHIRA VILLAGES.—OLENDA GIVES A GREAT BALL IN MY HONOR.—BEER-HOUSES.—GOATS COMING OUT OF A MOUNTAIN ALIVE.

SEVERAL days have elapsed since my arrival at Olenda. From more than one hundred and fifty villages of the plain, the people streamed to Olenda's town to see "the spirit." They came in the night, slept on the ground outside the town, and in the morning crowded about me, wondering at my hair, at my clothes, at my shoes; declaring that my feet were like elephant's feet, for they did not see the toes; and they would try to get a glance at my eyes. The moment I looked at them they ran off screaming, and especially the women and children. The Africans had a great dread of my look. They believe in the *evil eye*, and often, when I would look steadily at them, my best friends, with a shudder, would beg me not to do it.

So I may say that since my arrival the time has been devoted to seeing and being seen. And I assure you it was no joke to hear that uproarious crowd and their wild shouts—to have always in my sight a crowd of people yelling at every movement I made.

I had a Yankee clock, which was an object of constant wonder to them. They thought that there was a kind of spirit inside that made the noise, and that watched over me. Its constant ticking, day and night, was noticed, and they had an idea that the noise could never stop. At night of course the sound is louder, and this frightened them, and not one dared to come close to my hut.

Every day Olenda beats his kendo; every day he comes to get a look at me.

This Ashira prairie seemed to be shut in on all sides by mountains, which of course were covered with forest. Fancy the forest a sea of trees, and the Ashira Land an island. Pine-apples grew in great abundance, and thousands and thousands of them were clustered close together, and formed otôbi (prairies) by themselves.

This plain is the finest and most delightful country I had thus far seen in the jungle. The undulations of the prairie, which is a kind of table-land surrounded on every side by high mountains, gave the landscape a charming variety. The surrounding mountains, the splendid peak of the Nkoomoo Nabouali on the north, said by the superstitious Ashiras to be inhabited by satyrs like men; the Andelè and Ofoubou-Orèrè to the south, and the Ococoo to the east, are all covered with dense masses of foliage. In those forests are living tribes of wild men and wilder beasts, roaming at pleasure.

I have arrived in a country where I could see grass, and see distinctly the moon, the stars, and the sun without first being obliged to cut the trees down. Oh, you have no idea how nice it is to see an open space after you have been shut up in the forest for years.

From Olenda's village I made excursions all over the Ashira country. The villages were so numerous I could not count them. There were from one hundred and fifty to two hundred of them. Some were quite small, others were quite large; and what beautiful villages they were. I had not seen such pretty ones before. The houses were small, but the neatest I had met in the jungle. They are built generally in one long street, houses on each side. The streets are kept clean; and this was the first tribe I met where the ground at the back of the houses was also cleared off. In most villages there was, back of the houses, a street where great numbers of plantain-trees and some lime-trees, for they love lemons, were growing. The villages are surrounded by thousands of plantain-trees, and regular footpaths connected one village with another.

Ball after ball was given to me, and one evening Olenda gave me a very fine, big one. More than fifty drums beat, besides there were musicians armed with short sticks, with which they pounded with all their might on pieces of board. The singing was extraordinary, and the Ashira belles cut any amount of capers, one time raising their legs one way, then bending their bodies backward and forward, shaking their heads from one side to the other, kicking their heels together, the iron or brass bracelets or anklets adding to the harmony of *the musical instruments* I have described to you. The singing was as wild as can be imagined. Olenda's wives—for his majesty was blessed with several scores of them—danced with fury.

They danced all night, and the next morning there was a general stampede to the beer or cider-house. I must tell you that the Ashira are very fond of plantain wine.

I followed, for I wanted to see a beer-house and a general Ashira spree.

After walking for half an hour we came to a cluster

of trees, in the centre of which we found a brewery. A few women had charge of the premises—the wives of some of the Ashira.

What a sight presented itself to my view! There hung all round hundreds of large bunches of plantain in different stages of ripening, from the dark green to the

DRINKING PLANTAIN BEER.

bright yellow, hanging from the limbs of trees. There were also some red-skin plantains.

It was a large building, under a single roof, supported by numerous wooden pillars, and on these hung a great many bunches of plantain. In the middle of the building there were scores of large jars, manufactured in the country, some of which would hold ten or fifteen gallons. From the necks of some of them a quantity of rich white froth was running out. The beer in others was just ripe, and ready for drinking. There were also many large mugs, looking more like dishes, however, for the plantain juice to be poured into.

Very soon the men seated themselves, either on the stools that belonged to them or on mats, and the drinking began. Mug after mug was swallowed by each man. I think no German could drink the same amount of liquid. They became, after a while, jolly and boisterous; they began, in fact, to get tipsy.

Do not believe they were drinking at random. Each jug of wine belonged to several men, who had clubbed together; that is to say, each had given a certain amount of plantain to make the beer which the vessel contained.

The plantain with which the beer or wine is made is a kind of banana, much larger and coarser, and used, as you have seen, as food; but it must be cooked, the natives cooking it when it is green. When ripe, it is yellow like the banana.

The beer is made in the following manner: The plantain must be quite ripe; then it is cut in small pieces, which are put into the jar until it is half filled; then the jar is filled with water. After a few days it ferments; then the froth comes out, and the beer is ready for use.

The bunches of plantain, which were hanging by hundreds, had their owners, and had been brought from the plantations by their wives, and were ripening in the shade. As the plantations yield fruit all the year round, the beer is never lacking among the Ashiras.

After they were sufficiently excited, they began to talk of their wonderful warlike exploits, and I do believe it was who should lie the most. The greater the lie, the louder the applause.

I tasted the plantain beer, and found it somewhat sour; I did not like it at all.

I spent the day in the beer-house, and, when we returned to the village, the men insisted on having another dance, and they kept hard at work at it all night, and went all to sleep the next morning. I was glad when every thing was over, for my head began to ache.

I determined to visit the mountains from which the River Ofoubou takes its name. King Olenda was to take charge of my luggage, and I took only a few presents for the Ashira chiefs I was to see, and who had come to see and invite me to visit their towns in the mountains.

One of Olenda's sons was chief of our party, and Adouma, Quengueza's nephew, led with him. We did not start before old King Olenda had told all his people to take great care of the "spirit."

We left the village in the midst of the wildest shouts, and then wended our way through the beautiful green grass. Within a mile and a half south from Olenda we came to the foot of Mount Nchondo, one of the highest points of the prairie. There we all stopped; why, I could not guess.

When one of the Ashiras said to me, pointing to the mountain, "You see that mountain, Moguizi?" "Yes," said I. "From that part of the mountain," continued Oyagui, Olenda's great-grandson, in the most serious manner, "goats come out. That is a great mountain; a spirit lives there. Sometimes, when our people want a goat, they will go there, and a goat will come to them." I said, "That can not be." "Yes," insisted Oyagui, "I know plenty of people who get goats there."

Then we passed by numerous villages, skirting most

of the hills at their base, and crowds of people everywhere cried out, "The moguizi is coming! the moguizi is coming!"

All these villages were surrounded by groves of plantain and banana trees.

After a journey of about ten miles, we came, at the foot of the cloud-capped Mount Andelè, to the village of Mouendi, whose chief, Mandji, came forth with great joy to meet me, for he was a great friend of Adouma. He sang, as he came forward with his people, "It is good that the moguizi comes to see our town."

To the rear of the village, on the slope of the mountain, the forest had been cleared, and the space occupied by plantations, where tobacco, peanuts, plantains, yams, and sugar-cane were grown to an extent which makes this a land of plenty where no man starves. Bushes of wild cotton were seen now and then, but not in great numbers.

I was glad that I had reached a country where I should not readily starve—plantains and goats were plentiful. As I stood and cast my eyes over the scene, the yellow waving grass, with now and then a dark green patch in low land between the hills, where water stood, and the cane-fields contrasting with the dark green of the forest, reminded me of rural scenes at home; but I looked in vain for cattle; none were to be seen.

I had a great time at Mouendi; Mandji, its chief, was very kind to me. I had more goats and plantains given to me than my men and myself could eat. The Goumbi people were in great glee; that was just the country for them, and, I may now say it, it was just the country for me also. I was in clover, I thought.

CHAPTER XXV.

ASCENSION OF THE OFOUBOU-ORÈRÈ AND ANDELÈ MOUNTAINS.—THE ASHIRA BLEED THEIR HANDS.—STORY OF A FIGHT BETWEEN A GORILLA AND A LEOPARD.—THE GORILLA AND THE ELEPHANT.—WILD BOARS.

The day arrived when we were to ascend the Ofoubou-Orèrè and Andelè Mountains, which were the highest peaks of that range. Mandji, who is really a nice chief, had given me the necessary people, and I longed to reach the summits of these woody regions. We intended to hunt there also while we looked around.

Every one prepared himself for several days' hard work, and finally, when every thing was ready, each being loaded with a good stock of provisions, we bade good-by to the villagers.

The Ashiras, before starting, covered themselves with fetiches, as usual, and drew blood from their hands by cutting small gashes on them, in order to insure good luck in the hunt. They were in great spirits, for the idol of the village had told the people that we should kill much game. The first night after we camped a tremendous tornado blew from the northeast, leaving us safely in our leafy shelter, however, and then the men began to tell stories of the gorilla.

Oyagui was the first to get up. He was a splendid story-teller; but, before he began, he swore that he was going to tell a true story, part of which he saw, and a part was seen by his brother, which was the same as if he himself had seen it. A smile stole over the faces of all present, for Oyagui was known to tell tremendous big stories, and a great deal of faith was required before one could believe them.

"One day," said he, "a gorilla was walking in the forest, when he met a ngègo (leopard). The gorilla stopped, and so did the leopard. The latter, being hungry, crouched for a spring at his foe, whereat the gorilla set up a hideous roar. Undismayed by that terrific noise, the leopard made his leap, but was caught in mid air by the gorilla, who seized him by the tail, and whirled him round his head till the tail broke off and remained in his hand, and the animal escaped, leaving his brush in the big hands of the gorilla. How funny the leopard did look, as he ran off without his tail!"

"You never saw that," exclaimed one of the party.

"I did," said Oyagui; "I did, as sure as I live. The leopard ran away to his companions, who, when they saw him, asked, 'What is the matter?' whereupon the unfortunate beast recounted his defeat."

"How do you know," said another, "that the leopards asked the one without a tail 'What is the matter?' You can not understand leopard talk."

"Oh," said Oyagui, undismayed, "they looked at each other, and I am sure they said what I have told you, or something of the kind, for immediately the chief ngègo began howling till all the leopards of the forest came, who, when they saw their brother thus injured, and without a tail, vowed vengeance, and set out to find the gorilla. This my brother saw," said Oyagui, talking louder than ever, "and he followed the leopard, while I was watching the gorilla."

"They had not long to hunt. When the gorilla saw them coming he broke down a tree, of which he made a club, and then swung it round and round his head, keeping the troop of leopards at bay. At last, however, the gorilla grew tired, his efforts began to slacken, and he whirled round his tree with less force. He stopped, and then the leopards rushed on him with one accord, and soon killed him. They sprang on his head, on his breast, on his arms, and on his legs."

"You never saw this!" shouted all the Ashiras together.

"I have!" bawled Oyagui, as loud as he could.

Then they all said, "Oyagui, tell us another story." There was a pause and a short silence while we gave another start to the fires, for, at any rate, Oyagui had succeeded in making us think of leopards in telling us his story. Then Oyagui began again.

"A great gorilla was once walking in the forest with his wife and baby, when they came upon a huge elephant, who said, 'Let me pass, gorilla; move off, for these woods belong to me!'

"'Oh, oh!' said the gorilla, 'how do the woods belong to thee? Am I not the master here? Am I not the Man of the Woods? Do I not roam where I please?'"

"Oh!" once more exclaimed the Ashiras, "this can not be, for you do not talk gorilla; you can not understand gorillas' or elephants' talk."

"No," said Oyagui, "I can not understand gorillas' or elephants' talk, but I can see what they mean, for I have a fetich which makes me comprehend the talking of the beasts."

Oyagui continued:

"Ordering his wife and baby to move aside, the gorilla broke down a large limb of a tree, and, brandishing it like a club, made for the elephant, whom he soon killed by furious blows. The body of the latter I found a few days afterward, with the club of the gorilla lying by his side. I got frightened when I saw the big elephant charging at the gorilla, and the gorilla charging at the elephant, and so I ran away; but I saw the club by the side of the big elephant."

Soon after the conclusion of this story we went to sleep, I believing, for one, that Oyagui had most wonderful powers of imagination. I really do think that he believed all he said, for, as he told the stories, he got very excited, and his body shone with perspiration.

The next morning, after a good night's rest, I got up very early, and proceeded a little way into the forest, before our ascent, to see if I could find some antelope or gazelle, or some other kind of game, wandering about in search of food, when I unexpectedly heard the grunt of wild boars. I was alone. I listened, and made sure that they were coming down the mountain. I knew that I must get shelter in order not to be seen, for I had discovered that they were coming just in my direction. A wild boar would not be a bad thing, I thought, especially if it was fat. Were they yellow wild boars, or black ones? Yellow or black, one would be welcome.

Looking around, I saw the remains of a tree that had fallen down from old age. The top of the stump was about three feet above the ground, and in it was a hollow, into which I could easily get, and there could not be seen, for the tree, in falling, broke off, carrying away part of the trunk.

I looked inside to see if there were any snake, or scorpion, or centipede in it, but saw nothing.

If I had tried, I could not have made a better hiding-place. So I stepped in, making a peep-hole to see through, and lay in wait. The grunting became louder. I could hear them uprooting the ground, and finally four big yellow wild boars were before me. I cocked my gun

ATTACK ON THE WILD BOARS.

as the big fellow of the party approached, unaware of his danger, and fired, and down he came. His three companions made a leap of about ten yards—a tremendous leap it was. These wild boars can leap farther than an antelope. This was a *Potamocherus albifrons*, a species which I have described to you in a former volume.

There was great joy when I returned to the camp and

told the good news. They thought I had killed a monkey.

We had part of it for our breakfast, and it was excellent, but not very fat, as this time of the year is not their fat season.

One of my Ashira men had at home a small idol, which had the reputation of being an excellent guardian of his vacant house, and to this idol he was to take a piece of smoked boar's flesh. I succeeded in purchasing the idol, a likeness of which I here give you.

CHAPTER XXVI.

PROPOSE TO START FOR HAUNTED MOUNTAINS. — OLENDA SAYS IT CAN NOT BE DONE. — AT LAST I LEAVE OLENDA VILLAGE. — A TORNADO. — WE ARE LOST. — WE FIGHT A GORILLA. — WE KILL A LEOPARD. — RETURN TO OLENDA.

I soon after returned to Olenda's village.

One day I said to Olenda, "Olenda, have you ever been to the Nkoumou-Nabouali?" The wrinkled old chief looked at me through his small eyes for some time without saying a word, and then he replied, "Moguizi, no living man has ever been to the top of those mountains."

"What kind of people live in those mountains?"

"No one lives there," said Olenda, "except a race of people whom you may perhaps see, but, as soon as you approach their abodes, they vanish away, and no one can tell which way they have gone, for no one can see them when they disappear; their villages are made only with branches of trees."

I remained silent a little while.

Then I said, "Olenda, I want to go there; I want to go to the very top of the Nkoumou-Nabouali—to the very top," I added, pointing out to him the highest blue peak I could see from his village—" to the highest top, so that I may look at all the country round." I thought to myself what a glorious sight it would be, for, at a single glance, I should see hills, and plains, and rivers spread all around. My enthusiasm was very great when thinking of these things. I felt strong—so strong that I thought it would be nothing to go through that belt of immense forest and climb those high mountains.

Olenda gave a quiet laugh, which I still recollect, for it came from his hollow chest, and, if I had believed in witchcraft, I should have certainly thought Olenda was a sorcerer. His people were afraid of him, for no one could understand how he could have lived so long; all the wives he had married when a young man had died long ago; there was not a living man or woman in the country who knew him when he was a young man. The mothers of these people he knew when they were babies.

After he had given that laugh, which ended in a sarcastic smile, he looked me in the face and said, "You can not do it. No one has ever been there; there is a mighty spirit living in those woods which prevents people from passing. Besides, there is nothing to eat; there are no wild beasts, no antelope, no wild boar. At the foot of the mountain there is a tremendous waterfall, which drowns the roar of the gorilla."

"I must go," said I. So I talked to the Ashiras, and finally I managed, by making presents and promising more on my return, to get guides enough among the Ashira freemen to lead me through the impenetrable forests which lay between the prairie and the mountain top.

Then we prepared ourselves for the journey. I had two fine axes, which I filed and ground on soft stone in order to make them very sharp; also several *manchettes*, or cutlasses, to help us to cut our way through the jungle. I had several boxes of matches to light our fires, besides fire-steel and flints, in case our matches should get wet. I also took several wax candles, as it is much more easy to light the fires with them. Likewise I took one heavy blanket, for I knew not what kind of weather we should have on the mountains; as for my men, the fires would be their blankets.

The heavy portion of our luggage was several hundred bullets, about fifty pounds of shot with which to kill Guinea-fowls and other birds, and about ten pounds of powder.

For food we had smoke-dried plantains, which had been cooked first, and then dried on an orala by smoking them. We had also smoked cassada. This kind of food, prepared in this way, would keep much longer and be much lighter, so each man could carry a much greater quantity of it. We wanted plenty of food. It was the first time I had seen plantain prepared in that way.

We started in the midst of the cheers of the Ashira people, and, as we disappeared down the hill, I saw Olenda looking after us with his body half bent, and for all the world like some being of another planet.

We took a northerly direction till the afternoon, when we left the prairie, and entered at once into as fine a piece of bog land as any one could wish to be in. It was awful traveling; the ground was soft, and every step we made took us almost knee-deep into it. Now and then I had to look at my compass to see that we were going in the right direction, for there was no path whatever; but the Ashira said we would find one after passing the marshes; that it was a hunting-path, and that there we would meet game. The fellows were already thinking of meat.

When night came on we stopped on a hill surrounded

by bog; we were so tired that we had not the strength to build our shelters; besides, there were no large leaves to be seen. We lighted tremendous fires, but toward midnight I was awakened by the sound of distant thunder, which gradually grew louder and louder; then flashes of lightning glared through the forest, and then terrific claps of thunder rolled along the sky. The rain began to pour down with a fury that flooded the country in a short time; our beds of leaves were saturated, compelling us to get up. The rain kept pouring down with increasing violence. We had not built our fires sufficiently high, although we had used huge pieces of wood that ought to have been high enough from the ground to prevent the rain from putting them out. But they were getting dimmer and dimmer, and at last we were left in complete darkness. It was pitch dark, and we could not even see each other except when a flash of lightning would brighten the forest.

We were in a pretty fix. I began to regret that we had not been more careful. Leopards and other wild beasts might be prowling about, and get hold of some of us. What would the Ashiras say if one of their number should be carried away by a wild beast? They would call me a bad spirit.

We could not even talk, for the thunder was too loud, and drowned our voices; besides, the rain made a great noise as it fell in torrents upon the trees, and from their leaves to the ground. We were surrounded by tall trees, and I was afraid that some of them might be struck by the lightning, and their heavy broken limbs fall in the midst of us.

In fact, it was as uncomfortable a night as any one

could wish to spend in the jungle, for we knew not what would happen next. Toward four o'clock in the morning the rain ceased, but then I was wet to the bones; of course, my Ashiras would soon dry. We lighted our fires once more, having split in two some pieces of half-rotten logs which lay near by, and had perhaps lain there for more than a hundred years, the heart being soft and dry. This is the kind of wood we use to light our fires with when there has been a heavy rain, and the wood that has fallen from the trees is wet outside. In these immense forests, which have been resting in their gloomy solitude for ages, the growths of trees succeed one after the other. I have often wondered how Africa looked before it was covered with this dense vegetation, and what kind of animals it had, for the fauna of that country must have changed like ours. I remembered that once the immense mastodon roamed through America. With these thoughts I went to sleep in clothes wet to the skin. I took a large dose of quinine, however, in order to prevent a chill, which probably might have ensued from such a severe night.

The next morning I dried my wet clothes, and once more we went bravely into the great jungle, still taking by my compass a northerly direction through the dense and thorny forest. The hunting-path was almost a myth, for only now and then would we get a glimpse of it; but my Ashira men seemed to know almost every large tree we passed. We advanced slowly, our manchettes helping to cut the undergrowth. The third day I lost my only shirt—at least it would not hold together; and one of the legs of my pantaloons was torn off once, and I had to mend it with the fibre of the bark of trees. I lost, besides, many patches of skin, and the sharp thorns tore my flesh. Snakes we would see now and then.

We had hardly entered the jungle that first morning before I heard the roar of the gorilla. This at once revived my drooping spirits, as also those of my men, who immediately began to see looming up before them large pieces of gorilla meat broiled or roasted on charcoal.

A dead silence among ourselves followed the roar of the big monster. Each Ashira, as if by instinct, came close to me for protection. We had not far to go. I went off in an easterly direction with friend Gambo, leaving all the Ashiras together in fear of the gorilla. We had barely gone a quarter of a mile in the direction from whence the roar proceeded when we heard what was now a much louder roar, this time quite near. We stood quite still, for fear of alarming the beast, which was evidently approaching us unawares. At last we could see the bushes bend toward us. Gambo and I looked at each other, and inspected our guns; they were all right. A feeling of safety crept over us of course, for a good gun, with a steady aim, is a friend in need, and this we thought each of us possessed.

The fear of alarming the gorilla, however, proved needless. He had come where he had heard a noise, and when he saw us he at once struck the intervening bushes, rose to an erect position, made a few steps in a waddling sort of way, stopped, and seated himself; then beating his vast breast, which resounded like an old drum, he advanced straight upon us. His dark gray sunken eyes flashed with rage; his features worked convulsively; his intensely black face looked horrid. His huge canines, powerful sinewy hands, and immense arms told us that we must not expect mercy from the monster. At every few paces he stopped, and, opening his cavernous mouth, gave vent to his thunderous roars, which the forest gave back with multiplied echoes until it was full of the din.

He was evidently not a bit alarmed, but quite ready for a fight. We stood perfectly still. He advanced till he stood beating his breast within about six yards of us, when I thought it time to put an end to the scene. My shot hit him in the breast, and he fell forward on his face, dead. The gorilla seems to die easy if shot in the right place. This one proved to be a middle-aged male, and a very fine specimen, but it was utterly impossible to preserve his skin in that great jungle.

In a short time all the Ashira joined us, and soon after the gorilla was cut to pieces, the hands and feet being thrown away, and the brain being religiously preserved for fetiches.

There was plenty in the camp, for during the day I killed a nice little ncheri (gazelle), when I also had a feast.

We were now fairly in the midst of high hills, sometimes going down, then going up; but, to save me, I could not tell exactly where we were going. Occasionally we followed the tracks that elephants had made, but finally lost them. The elephants had evidently often changed their minds, and retraced their steps from whence they came. I could not tell exactly where the mountains of the Nkoumou-Nabouali were. The compass became of no use, for we never followed two minutes the same direction. At the rate we should have had to go through the forest, taking our course by the compass, we should have required perhaps a month or more, as we would have had to go on without making use of the clearings that we found now and then, or the tracks made by the wild beasts, or the little streams that came down from the hills. In fact, we would have had to make a road. The woods were very dense, game was scarce, and at last we had but one day's provisions left. The berries were not plentiful—indeed, for two or three days we did not eat to our heart's content for fear of running through our provisions too fast.

I had with me only the suit of clothes I wore and a spare pair of pantaloons, for I was getting very poor, and my stock of garments left at Olenda was small—indeed, it was so small that it was next to nothing. My poor rags could hardly be kept together. At times we had to pass through dense and very thorny jungles, where briers were as thick as grass on a prairie, and the holes in my clothes left so many bare spots that at every advance my scratched body bore witness of the hard time we had had, and of the difficulties we should encounter if I persisted in advancing into these mountains where there were no paths.

It came into my head that the Ashiras did not want to go; so I called our men together, and, after lighting a bright fire, we talked over "the situation," and then concluded that we had better return rather than risk certain death by starvation.

We rested that night in the forest, and the next morning I gave the order to return, feeling quite disappointed at my non-success. We set out praying only that we might not starve. We still were in good spirits, and laughed over our misfortune, although hunger began to pinch us hard, and I can assure you it is not a very pleasant thing. We were looking for berries every where, and the Ashiras for rat-holes and mice-nests, for mice and rats are great dainties among them; squirrels and monkeys, wild boars and antelopes, Guinea-fowls, parrots, and even serpents, but nothing was to be seen. To make it worse, we lost our way. We had been careless in not breaking boughs of trees when we followed the elephant's tracks, and we got into the wrong track of other elephants. Once lost in such a forest, the more you try to find your way the more you generally get bewildered. At last I took my compass, and we directed our steps, with its help, toward the south.

On a sudden, a cry of joy came from the Ashira. A bee's hive had been discovered by one of the men. He pointed us to a big tree. "Look," said he, "just where the branches start from the trunk. Don't you see bees round there? There is a big hole there, and the bees have their hive in it." As we saw the spot we all cried out, "Yes, there is a bee-hive."

Immediately the tree was ascended, the bees smoked, not out, but in, for we wanted plenty of food; the combs were brought down, for the man who ascended the tree had provided himself with large leaves and native cords to put the honey in, which he did, tying several parcels round his neck. As soon as he came down I put my hands on my revolvers and said, "I would blow out the brains of any one who should touch the honey before I gave it to him." So every thing was put before me. I unfolded the large leaves, divided the honey in exactly equal portions for each of us, not forgetting to put in the mixture the dead smoked bees, the worms, the comb, the honey, and the dirt that was among it, for in that way we had more of it. It was delicious! perfectly splendid! dead bees, honey, wax, dirt, worms, went down as fast as we could possibly eat them, and when done, I declared, "I wish, boys, we had more of this honey." This suggestion of mine was responded to by a vigorous hurra, all shouting, Rovano! rovano! "That is so, that is so."

We got up after our meal, all feeling rather the better for it. I said to myself, as I rose and felt a good deal more elasticity in my legs, "After all, honey eaten in the way we have done is far more strengthening than fine honey, that is so clear and clean." It is wonderful, Young Folks, how a few days of starvation sharpens the appetite. You can not understand it till you have gone through the ordeal of hunger.

In the afternoon, just after descending a hill, we came to a very thick part of the forest. We were all silent, for we wanted to kill game, when suddenly one of the men close to me made us a sign to stop and keep perfectly still, his face showing excitement and fear. I stopped and looked at him. Without saying a word, he pointed me to a tree. I looked, and could see nothing; I was looking at the wrong tree. He came close to me, and whispered the word ngègo (leopard). I looked in the direction indicated. Truly there was a magnificent leopard resting flat on the immense horizontal branch of a tree not more than fifteen or twenty feet from the ground.

We had narrowly escaped, for we had to pass under that tree. The leopard had seen us, and was looking at us, as if to say, "Why do you disturb me in my sleep?" for I suppose, as they move but seldom in the daytime, he intended to remain there for the day. His long tail wagged; he placed himself in a crouching position, ready to spring on some of us, hoping, I dare say, thus to secure his dinner. His glaring eyes seemed to look at me, and, just as I thought he was ready to spring, I fired between his two eyes, and the shot went right through his head, and down he fell with a heavy crash, giving a fearful groan. He tried to get up again, but another shot finished him, and then the tremendous war-shouts of the Ashiras rang through the forest. I shot that leopard at a distance of not more than eight or ten yards.*

The leopard was hardly on the ground before we rushed in with our knives. A heavy blow of the axe partly severed his head from his neck. We cut off his tail to take it back to town, and then took his claws off, to give them to Olenda for a necklace. The leopard was cut in pieces, and we lighted a big fire, or, rather, several big fires.

This leopard was fat—very fat, but smelt very strong—awfully so. The ribs looking the best, I thought I would try them and have some cutlets—real leopard cutlets. I flattened them and pounded them with the axe in order to make them tender. By that time the fire had burned up well, so I took from it a lot of bright burning charcoal, and put my cutlets on it. The cutlets soon afterward began to crisp; the fat dropped down on the charcoal, and a queer fragrance filled the atmosphere round. Then I put on the cutlets a little salt I had with me, rubbed them with some Cayenne pepper, and immediately after I began to go into them in earnest. The meat

* See Frontispiece.

was strong, and had an odor of musk, which was very disagreeable. I found it so at the third cutlet, and when I had done I took some salt in my mouth, mixed with Cayenne pepper, in order to see if I could not get rid of the taste; I could not. I wished then that the leopard had been some other animal.

This hard work, starvation, and wet at nights, began to tell upon me. Besides, I had made no discoveries, and I began to wish that I had listened to friend Olenda. His sarcastic and hollow laugh came back to me. His prophetic words, "I tell you, Moguizi, that no one ever ascended the Nkoumou-Nabouali," were remembered.

I began to feel weaker and weaker, and when I awoke two days after killing the leopard, I rose with difficulty from my bed of leaves. We set forward without breakfast. I dared not send men in the forest for berries; we must be contented with those we should find on our route, for every hour was precious, and they might not find any, after all. So we walked on with empty stomachs, longing for a sight of the Ashira country.

I could not be mistaken; my compass was in good order; I had taken into account its variation. We were going south, if not right straight, at least in a general southern direction.

On, and on, and on, through the gloomy jungle, no man saying a word to the other, and every man looking anxiously for the first sight of prairie-land, which, with my diseased brain, weakened by hunger, was to me like a fairy-land.

At last, on the afternoon of a day which I have never forgotten, a sudden lighting of the forest gloom told us that an open country was near at hand. With a certain renewal of strength and hope we set off on a run, caring not how the jungle would tear us to pieces, till we reached a village at the very bounds of the bush. Here the people were much alarmed at our appearance and our frantic actions. "Food! food! food!" shouted the Ashiras. That was all they could say. When they discovered that we did not mean mischief, they approached. The chief had seen me at Olenda, and he made haste with his people to supply our necessities with all manner of food in their possession—plantains, pine-apples, cassada, yams, fowls, smoked fish. The chief gave me a royal present of a goat, which we killed in the wink of an eye. I ate so much that I feared I should be ill from putting too large a share into my so long empty stomach.

We were so merry during that evening. I told the good old chief to come and see me at Olenda, and that I would give him a nice present there.

The next morning we reached Olenda. The old chief, of whom I did not wonder people were afraid, came to meet me at the entrance of the village, for we had been firing guns to announce our arrival, and, as soon as he saw me, he said, in his deep, hollow, and piercing voice, "Moguizi, no Ashira has ever been or will ever go to the top of the Nkoumou-Nabouali!"

My boy Macondai was very glad to see me again, and came with tears of joy to welcome me. The people were all pleased to see us.

A child, said to be a sorcerer, was bound with cords, and was to be killed the next day. After a great deal of talking to Olenda, the boy was not to be killed. I was glad I had come in time to save his life.

The weather by this time was getting oppressively

hot in the prairie. My long black hair was hanging too heavily on my shoulders. I wore it very long in order to astonish the natives. Every chief wanted me to give him a lock of my hair, and this they considered a very great present. They would immediately go to the Alumbi house to lay it at the foot of the idol, but more generally it was worn as a fetich.

I resolved to have my hair cut, as it was too long for comfort. I gave Makondai a large pair of scissors I had with me. Of course I did not expect him to cut my hair as a Fifth Avenue or fashionable hotel barber would do, the chief point being that he should cut it tolerably short. In the interior of Africa I was not obliged to bother myself about the latest style. Collars and neckties were unknown to me. When he had done he gathered up the hair and threw it in the street.

I was surprised some time after to hear a noise of scuffling and fighting, accompanied by awful shouting. I came out of my hut to see what was the matter. They were busily engaged in securing my hair, that the wind had scattered all around, each man picking up as much as he could, and trying to prevent his neighbor from getting any, so that he might have more to himself. Even old King Olenda was in the scramble for a share. He could not trust his people. He was afraid he would not get any if he depended upon them, and when I saw him he had a lock which his head wife had found for him. I never saw such a scramble for hair before; they looked and looked after a scattered hair all day, and when they gave up the search I am sure not a hair could have been found on the ground.

CHAPTER XXVII.

DEPARTURE FOR THE APINGI COUNTRY.—THE OVIGUI RIVER.—DANGEROUS BRIDGE TO CROSS.—HOW THE BRIDGE WAS BUILT.—GLAD TO ESCAPE DROWNING.—ON THE WAY.—REACH THE OLOUMY.

YONDER, in a northeasterly direction, lies a country where live a strange people called Apingi. The Ashira, who now and then visit the country, say that a large river flows through it, and that the river, which is called Ngouyai, runs also at the foot of the Nkoumou-Nabouali Mountains. On the banks of that large stream many strange tribes of men live, of whom they have heard, but have never seen.

Our evenings were often spent in talking about that strange country. It was said there was an immense forest between it and Ashira Land, and that there were paths leading to it through the jungle, which was believed to be very dense.

One morning I went to Olenda and said to him, "King, I wish to go to the Apingi country, and I want you to give me people to accompany me." The old man, with his little deep, sunken eyes, regarded me for a little while, for he seemed never tired of looking at me, then said, "Moguizi, you shall go to the Apingi country, and I will give you people who have been there to accompany you." And then he repeated his *kombo*, which I have given to you before, and returned to his hut.

K

If Olenda was not tired of looking at me, I must say that I was never tired of looking at him, for so old a person I had never seen in my life. I have often wondered if Olenda was not the oldest person living in the world. I believe he was.

When the king gave the order to get ready for my departure, great preparations were made. Food was collected and cooked for my trip, quantities of ripe plantain were boiled and then smoked, and then, the food being ready, the people came who had been ordered by the king to accompany me. Olenda gave me three of his sons, or, I should rather say, great-grandchildren. They were to be the leaders. Adouma, Quengueza's nephew, was the only stranger who was allowed to accompany me. This was a great favor, for the law was very strict in that land that no Commi should be permitted to go farther than the Ashira Land. Macondai was too small. I was afraid he would die from the hardships we should encounter in the jungle. Olenda was to take care of him.

The names of Olenda's three great-grandchildren were Minsho, Iguy, and Aiaguy. Minsho, being the eldest, was to be the chief.

It was a bad time of the year to start, for we were in the beginning of December. It rained every day, and tornadoes coming from that very Apingi country blew over us toward the sea. All the rivers were rising. In the valleys there was a great deal of water, but the prairie looked very green and beautiful. For the last few days it had been raining almost without intermission, and we had to delay our departure on account of the swollen state of the rivers.

But at last, on the 6th of December, 1858, there was a great commotion in the village of Olenda, for we were really about to start. Olenda had come out, and was surrounded by his people. He had called our party, and admonished his great-grandsons to take care of his moguizi, for the moguizi was his friend, and had come to him, Olenda. If Olenda had not been living, he would never have come into the country. The whole people shouted with one voice, "That is so." Then the old king proceeded formally to bless us, and to wish us good success, and that no harm should befall us on the road.

On this occasion his majesty was painted with the chalk or ochre of the Alumbi, and had daubed himself with the ochres of his most valiant ancestors, and with that of his mother. He invoked their spirits to be with us, and afterward took a piece of wild cane, bit off several pieces of the pith, and spat a little of the juice in the hand of each one of the party, at the same time blowing on their hands. Then, in his sonorous and hollow voice, which hardly seemed human, he said, solemnly, "Let all have good speed with you, and may your road be as smooth (pleasant) as the breath I blow on your hands."

Then Minsho received the cane, of which he was to take great care, as, if it were lost, heavy misfortunes would happen to us, but as long as he kept it all would be well. Minsho was to bring back the cane to Olenda.

Immediately after this we started, taking a path leading toward the northeast. The prairie in the valleys was very swampy, the heavy rains having overflowed the lands, and we had to walk through considerable pools of standing water. In one of these swamps we had to wade up to our waists in muddy water, and several of the party slipped down and seated themselves in a manner they did not like, to the great merriment of the others, whose turn was to come next, and who, when laughing at their neighbors' misfortunes, fancied they could go through safely. As for myself, being short in stature, I had the water on several occasions higher than my waist.

Toward noon we approached the Ovigui River, a mountain torrent which had now swollen into a river, and before reaching its natural banks we had to pass through a swamp in the forest for half an hour. The torrent had overflowed, and its waters were running swiftly down among the trees. I began to wonder how we were to cross the bridge. The Ashiras had been speaking of that bridge, and, in fact, we had delayed our start two or three days because they said the waters were too high.

At last we came to a spot where the ground was dry, and a little way farther I could see the swift waters of the Ovigui gliding down with great speed through the forest. I saw at once that even an expert swimmer would be helpless here, and would be dashed to pieces against the fallen trees which jutted out in every direction. Not being a very good swimmer, I did not enjoy the sight. There was one consolation, no crocodile could stand this current, and these pleasant "gentlemen" had therefore retired to parts unknown.

I wanted all the time to get a glimpse of the bridge, but had not succeeded in doing so. I called Minsho, who pointed out to me a queer structure which he called the bridge. It was nothing but a creeper stretched from one side to the other.

Then Minsho told me that some years before the bed

of the river was not where we stood, but some hundred yards over the other side. "This," he said, "is one of the tricks of the Ovigui." I found that several other of these mountain streams have the same trick. Of course Minsho said that there was a muiri (a spirit) who took the river and changed its course, for nothing else could do it but a spirit. The deep channel of the Ovigui seemed to me about thirty yards wide. Now in this new bed stood certain trees which native ingenuity saw could be used as "piers" for a bridge. At this point in the stream there were two trees opposite each other, and about seven or eight yards distant from each shore. Other trees on the banks were so cut as to fall upon these, which might have been called the piers. So a gap had been filled on each side. It now remained to unite the still open space in the centre, between the two "piers," and here came the tug. Unable to transport heavy pieces of timber, they had thrown across this chasm a long, slender, bending limb, which they fastened securely to the "piers." Of course no one could walk on this without assistance, so a couple of strong vines (lianas) had been strung across for balustrades. These were about three or four feet above the bridge, and about one foot higher up the stream.

I could barely see the vine, and my heart failed me as I stood looking at this breakneck or drowning concern. To add to the pleasurable excitement, Minsho told me that, on a bridge below, half a dozen people had been drowned the year before by tumbling into the river. "They were careless in crossing," added Minsho, "or some person had bewitched them." The waters of the Ovigui ran down so fast that looking at them for any length of time made my head dizzy. I was in a pretty fix. I could certainly not back out. I preferred to run the risk of being drowned rather than to show these

CROSSING THE OVIGUI RIVER.

Ashira I was afraid, and to tell them that we had better go back. I think I should never have dared to look them in the face afterward. The whole country would have known that I had been afraid. The moguizi would have then been nowhere. A coward I should have been called by the savages. Rather die, I thought, than to have such a reputation.

I am sure all the boys who read this book would have had the same feelings, and that girls could never look at a boy who is not possessed of courage.

The engraving before you will help to give a good idea of the bridge I have just described to you, and of our mode of crossing.

The party had got ready, and put their loads as high on their backs as they could, and in such a manner that these loads should slip into the river if an accident were to happen. The crossing began, and I watched them carefully. They did not look straight across, but faced the current, which was tremendous. The water reached to their waists, and the current was so swift that their bodies could not remain erect, but were bent in two. They held on to the creeper and advanced slowly sideways, never raising their feet from the bridge, for if they had done otherwise the current would have carried them off the structure.

One of the men slipped when midway, but luckily recovered himself. He dropped his load, among the articles in which were two pairs of shoes; but he held on to the rope and finished the "journey" by crossing one arm over the other. It was a curious sight. We shouted, "Hold on fast to the rope! hold on fast!" The noise and shouting we did was enough to make one deaf.

Another, carrying one of my guns, so narrowly escaped falling as to drop that, which was also swept off and lost. Meantime I wondered if I should follow in the wake of my shoes and gun. At any rate, I was bound to show the Ashira that I was not afraid to cross the bridge, even, as I have said, at the risk of being drowned. It would have been a pretty thing to have these people believe that I was susceptible of fear. The next thing would have been that I should have been plundered, then murdered. These fellows had a great advantage over me. Their garments did not trouble them.

At last all were across but Minsho, Adouma, and myself. I had stripped to my shirt and trowsers, and set out on my trial, followed by Minsho, who had a vague idea that if I slipped he *might* catch me. Adouma went ahead. Before reaching the bridge I had to wade in the muddy water. Then I went upon it and marched slowly against the tide, never raising my feet, till at last I came to the tree. There the current was tremendous. I thought it would carry my legs off the bridge, which was now three feet under the water. I felt the water beating against my legs and waist. I advanced carefully, feeling my way and slipping my feet along without raising them. The current was so strong that my arms were extended to their utmost length, and the water, as it struck against my body, bent it. The water was really cold, but, despite of that, perspiration fell from my face, I was so excited. I managed to drag myself to the other side, holding fast to the creeper, having made up my mind never to let go as long as I should have strength to hold on. Should my feet give way, I intended to do like the other man, and get over by crossing one arm over the other. At last, weak and pale with excitement, but outwardly calm, I reached the other side, vowing that I would never try such navigation again. I would rather have faced several gorillas, lions, elephants, and leopards, than cross the Ovigui bridge.

Putting ourselves in walking order again, we plunged into the great forest, which was full of ebony, barwood, India-rubber, and other strange trees. About two miles from the Ovigui we reached a little prairie, some miles long and a few hundred yards wide, which the natives called *Odjiolo*. It seemed like a little island incased in that great sea of trees.

What a nice little spot it would have been to build a camp under some of the tall, long-spread branches of trees which bordered it! But there was no time for camping. There were to be no stops during the daytime till we reached the Apingi country.

A few miles after leaving the Odjiolo prairie we came to a steep hill called Mount Oconcou. As we ascended we had to lay hold of the branches in order to help ourselves in the ascent, and we had to stop several times in order to get our breath. We finally reached a plateau from which we could see Nkoumou-Nabouali Mountains. Then we surmounted the other hills, with intervening plains and valleys, all covered with dense forest, and at last found ourselves on the banks of a most beautiful little purling mountain brook, which skirted the base of our last hill. This nice little stream was called the Aloumy or Oloumy. Here we lit our fires, built shelters, and camped for the night, all feeling perfectly tired out, and I, for one, thankful for the nice camp we had succeeded in building, for I needed a good night's rest.

CHAPTER XXVIII.

A GORILLA.—HOW HE ATTACKED ME.—I KILL HIM.—MINSHO TELLS A STORY OF TWO GORILLAS FIGHTING.—WE MEET KING REMANDJI.—I FALL INTO AN ELEPHANT-PIT.—REACH APINGI LAND.

THE next morning we felt much refreshed, and once more entered the forest, following a footpath which was sometimes good, but oftener very bad. The country became more rugged and mountainous. On every side we met beautiful little streams of water wending their way through the woods. Very often we had to march in the bed of some purling brook, as the easiest way we could find. This second day was exceedingly trying to our feet, for we made our way the greatest part of the time through a dense and gloomy forest. Several times we heard, at a great distance, the roar of the gorilla and the heavy footsteps of elephants. We heard also the cries of the nshiego-mbouvé, and now and then the shrill cry of a monkey.

In the afternoon I was startled by the roar of a gorilla, and it was three quarters of an hour before we came near him. He was then close to the path we were following, and roared incessantly. I find that I can not get accustomed to the roar of the gorilla, notwithstanding the number I have hunted and shot; it is still an awful sound to me. The long reverberations coming from his powerful chest, the vindictive bark by which each roar is preceded when about to attack, the hollow monotone of the first explosion, the ugly, ferocious look which he gives to his enemies, all are awe-inspiring, and proclaim the great beast the monarch of the forest of Equatorial Africa.

When we came near him, he, in turn, at once made toward us, uttering a succession of bark-like yells, denoting his rage, and reminding me of the inarticulate ravings of a maniac. Balancing his huge body with his arm, the animal approached us, every few moments stopping to beat his breast, and throwing his head back to utter his tremendous roar. His fierce, gloomy eyes glared upon us, the short hair on the top of his head was rapidly agitated, and the wrinkled face was contorted with rage. It was like a very devil, and I do not wonder at the superstitious terror with which the natives regard the monster.

His manner of approach gave me once more an opportunity of seeing with how much difficulty he maintains himself in an erect posture. His short legs are not able firmly to support the vast body. They totter beneath the great weight, and the walk is a sort of waddle, in which the long and prodigiously strong arms are used in a clumsy way to balance the body, and keep up the ill-sustained equilibrium. Twice he sat down to roar.

My gun had, of course, been loaded in the morning (I always took care to reload my guns each day), and could thus be depended upon, so I shouldered it, feeling easy. I waited till he was close enough, and then, as he once more stopped to roar, I delivered my fire, and brought him down on his face—dead.

His huge body proclaimed his giant strength. There is enough humanity in the beast to make a dead one an awful sight, even to accustomed eyes, as mine were by this time. It was as though I had killed some monstrous creature which had something of the man in it.

We could do nothing with the gorilla, so the Ashiras took as much meat out of his body as they could conveniently carry. We cut his head off and carried it with us. It was a huge and horrible head. Looking at his enormous canine teeth, I saw at once that the monster must have had a tremendous fight a year or two before, for one of them had been broken off in the socket of the jaw. What a grand sight it must be to see a gorilla fight! This reminded me of the stories I had sometimes heard from the natives regarding the fearful conflicts the male gorillas have among themselves for the possession of a wife. Indeed, the fight that this one was engaged in must have been a severe one, for not only had one of his large teeth been broken, but one of his arms was shorter than the other, and had evidently been broken and united again, not, I am sure, by a surgeon-gorilla, for I do not believe they have any, but nature and time were the healing processes. There is a skeleton of a gorilla in the British Museum, the arm of which had been broken, no doubt, in some conflict, but when the animal was killed the wound had healed, and the bones of the arm had united.

Minsho promised to tell us the story of a fight between two gorillas in the evening by the camp-fire.

How tremendous that blow must have been, I thought, in order to break that powerful muscular and thick-set bony arm! The forest must have been filled with the loud yells of the monster as he fought desperately against his enemy.

We continued our way after fording a stream about one hundred and twenty feet wide, called the Louvendji, carrying our gorilla's head with us, and toward dusk built our camp. After we had seated ourselves by the fireside, and I had taken my own modest meal, Minsho got up, after filling himself with gorilla meat, and said, " Moguizi, I promised you, after you had killed this big gorilla this morning, that I would tell you a gorilla story. Are you ready to hear it?" " I am ready to hear it," I said," and all the party shouted "All are ready to hear it."

" Long ago," said he, " before I was born, and in the time of my father—for the story I am going to tell you is from my father—there was a terrible gorilla fight in the woods. My father had been cutting down trees in the forest in order to make a plantation, and was returning home, when suddenly he heard, not far from him, the yells of gorillas, and he knew that the beasts were coming quickly toward him.

" Not far from where he stood there was a large hollow tree, into which he at once entered and hid himself, for he was afraid of the gorillas. He had with him only his axe, and of course could not dream of fighting the gorillas, especially as there were two of them. He had hardly entered his hiding-place before the gorillas made their appearance. My father trembled with fear lest they should discover where he was, but they were so enraged at each other that they did not busy themselves about what surrounded them."

Minsho was getting excited, and his eyes began to sparkle as he came to the fighting part of his story. There was a pause and a dead silence, for we wanted to hear about the fight of the two gorillas. Minsho suddenly gave a tremendous yell in the Ashira fashion. "Now," said he, "open your ears, for you are going to hear what my father saw.

"The two gorillas seized each other and rolled on the ground, yelling. One at last gave the other a bite, which made his enemy give an awful shriek of pain. They then got up, their faces covered with blood, their bodies lacerated, and, looking fiercely at one another with their deep-sunken eyes, each gave a yell of defiance, and both slowly advanced again; then the larger, which was probably the elder, stopped, both wanting rest in order to breathe, and then they pounced upon each other, screaming, yelling, bellowing, beating their chests, retreating, and advancing. At last they both stood on their hind legs a few rods from each other, their eyes seeming to flash fire, and advanced once more for a deadly fight, when the older and bigger one raised his hand and gave his antagonist a most fearful blow, which broke the other's arm. Immediately the badly-wounded gorilla fled, leaving the old gorilla master of the field; but then the victor was also covered with blood. My father still trembled, for he was afraid of being discovered. After a time, when all was silent, he looked round, and saw that the victorious gorilla had also gone off."

By this time Minsho was covered with perspiration; he fancied, I suppose, that he had seen the fight himself. He concluded by saying, "I have no doubt the gorilla we killed this morning lost one of his big tusks in a great fight with another gorilla," in which opinion we all coincided.

After this story we lay down on our beds of leaves,

and, surrounded by blazing fires, all went to sleep, hoping to rest well, for we had a hard day's work before us on the morrow.

In the morning the songs of birds awoke us from our sleep. After roasting a ripe plantain and eating it, I started once more, following a path by which we traveled all day. Again no game was seen; we did not even meet the footsteps of an elephant; and a little before sunset we came to a bando or olako, built by the Ashira and Apingi people especially for the convenience of travelers.

The bando was roofed with peculiar and very large leaves, here called the shayshayray and the quaygayray. Here we concluded to stop for the night. Not even the cry of an owl or of a hyena disturbed the stillness; no elephant's footstep came to awake us from our slumber; the howls of the leopard were not to be heard.

Several days had been thus spent in the jungle, but we were now compelled to hurry along, for we had no food. In the mean time we had a view of some small prairies, and in one of them had seen villages, which the Ashiras said were those of the Bakalai; but as Minsho and the rest of the Ashiras did not want to go near them, we re-entered the forest. "The Bakalai here," said Minsho, who I could see was not gifted with any great amount of bravery, "always stop and fight people." So we managed to pass their villages unseen.

Minsho said we were approaching the country of the Apingi. He was not mistaken. In the afternoon, while we were passing through dense woods, we heard people talking not far from us, and I came suddenly on a man who turned out to be Remandji, king of the Apingi.

At the sight of me he and his company stood silent

and amazed for a few minutes, when he began to dance about me in a most unroyal and crazy manner, shouting again and again, "The spirit has come to see me! the spirit has come to see my country!" He kept looking at me steadfastly, and for a while I thought his majesty had gone out of his mind.

King Remandji looked like a very fine old negro. The question that arose in my mind was, "How did the king happen to be in the woods?" His majesty had come to fish in a neighboring creek, for kings here are modest in their tastes, and was on his way to meet his wives, who had been sent on before him. He knew Olenda's sons, and directed them to a certain spot, and said he would be back that evening and bring his wives with him.

We parted with the king, rejoicing in the prospect of having fish and plantain for dinner. Meantime we went on, and when the evening came we all began to feel somewhat anxious about our quarters. Game was said to be plentiful in the forest, so I pushed a little out of the path, and, thinking I had seen something like a gazelle, I stepped forward toward it, when down into an elephant-trap I went, feeling quite astonished at finding myself at the bottom of it. It was a wonder my gun did not go off.

This trap I had fallen into was about ten feet deep, eight feet long, and six feet wide. As soon as I recovered sufficiently to comprehend my position, I began to holla and shout for help. No one answered me. I shouted and shouted, but no reply came. I was in a pretty fix. "Suppose," said I to myself, "that a huge snake, as it crawls about, should not see this hole, and tumble down on top of me." The very thought made me shout louder and louder. At times I would call, "Ayagui! Ayagui! Minsho! Minsho!" Finally I fired a gun, and then another, and soon I heard the voices of my men shouting "Moguizi, where are you? Moguizi, where are you?" "Here I am!" I cried. "Where?" I heard Minsho repeat. "Close by—here, Minsho, in a big elephant-pit; look out, lest you fall into it yourself." Minsho by this time knew where I was, and called all the men. They immediately cut a creeper and let it

THE ELEPHANT-TRAP.

down. I fired off my gun, and sent it up first, and then, holding fast to the creeper, I was lifted out of the pit, and very glad I was too, I assure you. The wonder to me was that I did not break my neck in getting into it.

Finally we reached the place where Remandji had directed Minsho to go. We lighted our fires, and soon after Remandji made his appearance. He looked again and again at me. His women were frightened, and did not show themselves. Happily, his majesty brought some plantains and fish with him.

I thought I had before known what musquitoes were, but I never saw the like of those we had in this spot. They certainly must have been a new kind, for their sting was like that of a bee, and very painful. Hundreds of them were buzzing around each one of us. My eyes, hands, and legs were swollen. I had a musquito-net with me, but inside of it they would get, how I could not tell. Several times I got out of the net, and when I thought I had shaken it well, and driven every one of them off, I would get under it again in the twinkle of an eye; but the musquitoes, which seemed perfectly famished, were like vultures, and would get in at the same time that I did. The Ashiras declared that they had never before seen such a place for musquitoes. Smoke and fire seemed to have no effect upon them. I never suffered such torture in my life. They beat all I had ever seen in the shape of musquitoes. The next morning I was so terribly bitten that I looked as if I had the measles or the chicken-pox.

Remandji, who had built his camp next to ours, came declaring that the people must have bewitched the place where we had slept, and off he took us to his village. After a three hours' march, we came at last, through a sudden opening in the forest, to a magnificent stream, the Rembo Apingi or Ngouyai. I stood in amazement and delight, looking at the beautiful and large river I had just discovered, and the waters of which were gliding toward the big sea, when a tremendous cheer from the Ashiras announced to the Apingi, Remandji's subjects, who had made their appearance on the opposite bank, that a spirit had come to visit them. The latter responded to the cheering, and presently a great number of exceedingly frail flat canoes and several rafts were pushed across, and soon reached our side of the river; they had come to ferry us over. The Apingi people live only on the right bank of this noble river.

I got into a very small canoe, which was managed with great skill by the Apingi boatman. I did not see how he could keep his equilibrium in the frail-looking shell.

The shouting on the Apingi side was becoming louder and louder, and when I landed the excitement was intense. "Look at the spirit!" shouted the multitude. "Look at his feet! look at his hair! look at his nose!" etc., etc.

They followed me till I was safely housed in one of the largest huts in the town, which was about twelve feet long and seven feet broad, with a piazza in front. When all my luggage was stored there was hardly room to move. I had indeed reached a strange country.

Presently Remandji came to me, followed by all the old men of his town and several chiefs of the neighboring villages. Twenty-four fowls were laid at my feet; bunches of plantains, with baskets of cassava. And Remandji, turning toward the old men, said, " I have beheld what our fathers never saw—what you and I never saw before. I bid thee welcome, O spirit! I thank your father, King Olenda," said he, turning to Minsho, " for sending this spirit to me." Then he added, " Be glad, O spirit, and eat of the things we give thee."

Whereupon, to my great astonishment, a slave was handed over to me, bound, and Remandji said, " Kill him; he is tender and fat, and you must be hungry."

I was not prepared for such a present. They thought I was a cannibal—an eater of human flesh—and there stood before me a fat negro, who during the night had been caught, for Remandji had sent word to the people of my coming, and in his forethought determined that I must have a good meal on my arrival.

Then I shook my head, spat violently on the ground, which is a great way of showing disgust, the people all the time looking at me with perfect astonishment. I made Minsho tell them that I abhorred people who ate human flesh, and that I, and those who were like me in the spirit-land, never did eat human flesh.

Just fancy! What a fine present! A nice fat negro, ready for cooking. It was like the presentation of a fat calf.

Remandji then said, " What becomes of all the people we sell, and that go down the river for you to take away? We hear you fatten them before they are killed. Therefore I gave you this slave, that you might kill him and make glad your heart."

A deep blush came over my face, I felt so ashamed. It was true, the white man had come into their country for hundreds of years and carried away their people.

After my refusal of the fat negro, who was glad to get free, Remandji's wives cooked the food for me which had before been presented. The king tasted of every thing that was laid before me, and drank of the water which was brought for me to drink. Such is the custom, for the people are afraid of poison; and the wife always tastes of the food she presents to her husband before he eats it, and the water he is going to drink.

The uproar in the village was something terrific. I

thought I should be deafened, and that their wonder at seeing me would never cease.

For a bed I had but a few sticks, but I was glad that night to lay upon them, and to have one of those little huts to shelter me from rain, for I had had a hard time, I can assure you, since I had left Olenda's.

Before going to sleep I thanked the kind God who had watched over me and led me safely into the midst of tribes of men whom no white man had ever seen before.

CHAPTER XXIX.

FIRST DAY IN APINGI LAND. — I FIRE A GUN. — THE NATIVES ARE FRIGHTENED. — I GIVE THE KING A WAISTCOAT. — HE WEARS IT. — THE SAPADI PEOPLE. — THE MUSIC-BOX.—I MUST MAKE A MOUNTAIN OF BEADS.

IN the morning when I awoke I looked round my room. Of course I did not have to look far, for the house was small; besides, it was filled with my baggage. Several fetiches hung on the walls, and in a corner was the skull of an antelope fastened to the roof. There were no windows, the floor of pounded yellow clay, and just by the few sticks which formed my bed were the remains of an extinguished fire. It was daylight, for I could hear the birds singing. The sun had risen, for I could see the sunshine through the crevices of the walls, which were made of the bark of trees, and through these the light came in. I listened to hear voices in the village; but no, all was silent. I got up, intending to go to the river to wash my face, and opened the door, which had been made with the bottom of an old canoe. Every hut in the village had its door, for there were famished leopards in the forest which often carried away people.

I had hardly stepped out of the house when I saw before me a very large crowd of people, who gave a loud yell at my appearance. I instinctively put my hand on one of my revolvers and held my gun in readiness; then looked at these people, who had been surrounding my hut since daylight, without saying a word.

Their yells were pretty loud. I knew not what they meant at first. I looked at them, when most of the women and children, and some of the men, ran away, although I cried out to them not to be afraid.

King Remandji soon arrived to say good-morning to me, and, while he was by my side, I raised the double-barreled gun I had with me, which I had loaded with a very heavy charge of powder, and fired it off. The gun recoiled on my shoulder, and hurt me slightly. The people fled in dismay, and the noise of the detonation re-echoed through the forest.

Remandji regarded me with fear and trembling. I reassured him by a smile, and by putting on his head a most flaming red cap which I had got ready for him. How he admired the bright red! He shouted to his people to come back, which they all did.

After washing my face in the river I returned to the village. It was a beautiful village. The houses were small, most of them being eight or ten feet long and six or eight feet wide. The walls were built with the bark of trees, and were about five feet high. The roofs were thatched either with large leaves or with the leaves of the palm, and at the top were about seven feet high. At the rear of the houses were large groves of plantain-trees.

Walking through the street, I came to the big idol, or mbuiti of the place, which stood under a ouandja (a covered roof), and there kept guard. That morning a few plantains, ground-nuts, sugar-cane, and a piece of a deer were before it. There was also a vessel with palm wine.

After walking to the end of the village I came back

to Remandji, the people hollaing and shouting all the time, "The good spirit has come! the spirit has come!"

I breakfasted outside of my hut, a few roasted plantains and a boiled fowl being my fare. How wild the shouts of these people were when they saw me eating! They were perfectly frantic. The fork was an object of the greatest wonder. They exclaimed, "The spirit does not eat with his hand; the spirit has a queer mouth; the spirit has teeth that are not filed sharp to a point; the spirit has a nose; how strange is the hair of the spirit!"

The crowd was pouring in from all the surrounding villages, and the excitement was intense. They were afraid, but, in despite of their fear, they came to see the great spirit who had arrived in their country.

After breakfast I called Remandji, and led him into my hut, and also the two head men, or graybeards of his village. Then I put on his majesty a flaming red waistcoat. I could not spare a coat, and I had no pantaloons to give him; luckily, they never want to wear the latter in this part of the world. He looked splendid with his waistcoat on. I also put round his neck a necklace of large blue and white beads, of the size of sparrow's eggs. I gave him, into the bargain, a looking-glass, and he was very much frightened when he saw his face in it, and he looked at me as if to say "What next?"

To the two elders, or graybeards, I gave each a necklace of large beads, and put on the head of each a red cap. Then we came out. As soon as the people saw them appear in such great style, they became very wild. I fired two guns, and Remandji and the two graybeards told the people not to be afraid. Immediately, guided by the same instinct, they all advanced toward us in a half-sitting posture, clapping their hands, and at the same time shouting "Ah! ah! ah!" When they thought they were near enough, they stopped, looked at me with a queer expression, and then shouted, "You are a great spirit! you are a great spirit!" and then they suddenly got up, and ran away to the other end of the village.

"Really the Apingi country is a strange land," said I to myself.

In the afternoon several thousand strangers filled the village. They had come to look at me, but before sunset almost all of them had returned to their homes. They had come by water and by land, from the mountains and from the valleys. The story of the arrival of the spirit in Remandji Village had spread far and wide, and every one came to see if it was true, desiring to see for themselves. But how afraid they were when I looked at them! How fast they ran away, and how quickly they would come back, but always keeping at a respectful distance!

In the evening there was a grand ball. The noise was horrible, the dancing was grand, the gesticulations and contortions were funny, the tam-tams sounded strangely, the singing was powerful, and I, of course, enjoyed the affair amazingly. I staid out all night to please them, and they were glad to see me look at them and laugh.

After a few days I became the great friend of a good many. I gave them beads, especially the women. I handled their little babies, and never got angry, though sometimes their curiosity annoyed me very much indeed.

Remandji and I became great friends. He was a real nice king, and we spent hours together. I was obliged to use Minsho as an interpreter, for I do not understand

L

the Apingi tongue very well. It seems to me like the language of the Mbinga, a tribe which I have spoken of in "Stories of the Gorilla Country."

One day a great crowd came and asked me to take my shoes off. When I asked them why, they said they wanted to know if I had toes like they had. "You have ears like we have," said they, "and we want to see if you have cloven feet like an antelope. We want to see if your feet are like those of a people who live far away from here, of whom we have heard, and who are called *Sapadi*. Yes," they exclaimed, with one voice, "far away in the mountains there are Sapadi; they do not have feet like other people; they have feet like antelopes; they have cloven feet."

I told them that there were no such people. Remandji immediately called one of his slaves, a man to whose country none of the Apingi had ever been (the Shimba country), and he declared positively, with a look of great truthfulness, that he had seen Sapadi. Another man also came forward and declared the same thing—they were people like the Apingi, only their feet were like those of antelopes.

To please them, I took off my boots. This was done in the midst of most vociferous cheers. They took my socks to be my skin. After my socks were taken off, and my naked feet burst upon their sight, the excitement became intense. The idol was brought out, the drums began to beat, and they sang songs to me, shouting and hollaing in the most approved African manner. Remandji took one of my feet in his lap and touched it, declaring that it was softer than the skin of a leopard. When his people saw this they became frantic. "The great spirit has come! the great spirit has come!" they shouted; "the king holds one of his feet!" Remandji rose, and, in a half-squatting position, danced and sang before me, the drums in the mean time beating furiously. The noise was deafening. They took me for a god.

When they had calmed down a little I went into my hut, wound up my large music-box, and, coming out, set it on an Apingi stool in the midst of the crowd, who immediately retreated farther off. I then let the spring go, and at once the music began to play. A dead silence followed the tumult; the drums dropped down from be-

THE MUSIC-BOX.

tween the drummers' legs; a leaf falling on the ground could have been heard; they were perfectly mute. Remandji and the people looked at me in affright. I went away, but of course the music continued to go on. They looked from me to the box, and back again, and finally exclaimed, "Lo! the devil speaks to him." I disappeared into the woods, and the music continued—the devil continued to speak.

The town is filled once more with strangers from the countries round, who have come to see the spirit that is stopping with Remandji. The forests are full of olakos in which these people sleep. The women appear hideously ugly; every one of them seems to have three or four children, and they are tattooed all over. On the bodies of many of them one could not find a spot as big as a pea that was free from this tattooing. They think that cutting their bodies in this way is beautifying. It is simply hideous. They file their teeth sharp to a point, which gives their faces a frightfully savage appearance; but, with all their ugliness, the Apingi were kind-hearted, always treated me well, and loved me. I always tried to do what was right by them.

One day they saw me writing my journal, and they said I was making print and cloth to give them. During the nights they all believed I did not sleep, but that I was at work making beads and all the things I gave them, whereupon ensued a great council of above thirty Apingi chiefs, who, after due deliberation with Remandji, who was at their head, came to me, surrounded by thousands of their people, and then their king delivered the following speech: "Spirit, you are our king; you have come to our country to do us good." The people, with one accord, repeated what Remandji had said—"You can do every thing." I wondered what was coming next. Then, in a loud voice, he added, "Proceed now to make for us a pile of beads, for we love the beads you make and give us. Make a pile of them as high as the tallest tree in the village," and he pointed to a giant tree which could not have been less than two hundred feet in height, "so that our women and children may go and take as many beads as they wish. You must give us cloth, brass kettles, copper rods, guns, and powder."

The people liked the speech of Remandji, and shouted "Yo! yo!" a sign of approval.

He continued: "The people will come to see you after you have gone; and when we shall say to them, 'The spirit who came has gone,' they will say, 'It is a lie! it is a lie! no spirit ever came to visit Remandji.' But when the whole country shall be filled with the things which we ask you to make, then, though they do not see you, they will say, 'Truly a spirit has visited the land of the Apingi, and lived in Remandji's village.'"

The faces of the crowd were beaming with satisfaction, for they approved of Remandji's speech. Then there was a dead silence again. I did not know what to say. I did not want to tell them I was a spirit, nor did I wish to tell them I was not one, for prestige is a great thing in a savage country.

They felt grieved when I told them I brought them things, and did not make them. They did not believe me, and said, "Thy spirit does not wish to do what we ask of it. Why, spirit, will you not do what we ask you!" and then the whole crowd began to dance and sing before me, saying, "Moguizi, do not be angry with us. Moguizi, we love you. Moguizi, you are good. Moguizi, stay with us."

On my continued refusal they scattered, and I went among them.

CHAPTER XXX.

A LARGE FLEET OF CANOES. — WE ASCEND THE RIVER. — THE KING PADDLES MY CANOE. — AGOBI'S VILLAGE. — WE UPSET. — THE KING IS FURIOUS. — OKABI, THE CHARMER. — I READ THE BIBLE. — THE PEOPLE ARE AFRAID.

REMANDJI and I had been talking of traveling together, and I had told him that I wished to ascend the river. He promised to have a fleet of canoes prepared, and that his people would turn out *en masse*.

He was as good as his word. The appointed day came. Quite a little fleet had been brought together. But what canoes! my goodness! what a difference between them and the canoes of the Commi country! They were very small—mere nut-shells. Remandji proudly pointed to the fleet he had collected to take me up. While he was talking to me I was thinking seriously of the great probability of capsizing, and the prospect was not exactly cheering, for the current of the river was strong. Though sometimes I have no objection to a ducking, I had strong objections to getting it in that manner, with all my clothes on.

Then the order for departure was given by the king. There was no help for it. I had asked canoes to go up. Remandji had done the thing in great style. I could not back out.

I was led in front of the royal canoe. Half a dozen

of these could have been easily put inside of one of Quengueza's canoes. The royal canoe was not much better than any other canoe, though the largest one had been chosen for me.

I made my preparations against accident—that is to say, ready in case we capsized. I tied my compass to a cord about my neck; then I tied my gun fast by a long rope to the canoe, which would float at any rate; and I had a small box of clothes, a shirt, and two pairs of shoes, which I tied also. I tied a handkerchief round my head, and put my watch inside on the top, so that it would not get wet.

There was not a host of people to go in the royal canoe—Remandji, a paddler, and myself—that was all. No more could get in with safety. There was not so much royalty and state as you see in the department of the navy. The admiral of the fleet I could not find.

Rafts are used extensively, but only for crossing the river or in going down the stream.

Each canoe has two or three men in it. How small they all were! quite flat on the bottom, and floating only a few inches above the water. They are very well designed for the swift current of the river, which runs, at this time of the year (December), at the rate of four miles an hour after a heavy rain.

Remandji was dressed in the flaming red waistcoat I had given him. The king paddled the canoe. As for me, I was perfectly satisfied to seat myself in the bottom, expecting all the time to upset, for steadiness was not part of our programme. I was quite uncomfortable, and as the canoe leaked, the part of my pantaloons upon which I was seated was a little more than damp; but no matter, it was cooling. But I could not help wishing the Apingi canoes at the bottom of the river; this hard wish of mine, of course, to be fulfilled when I should not be in one of them.

Remandji shouted with all his might to the fleet of small canoes to keep out of our way, for surely if a canoe had knocked against ours we should have been in the water before we had time to give the fellows our blessing.

We went gayly up the river, the royal canoe being ahead of all the others, Remandji and his man paddling as hard as they could. The people of the villages we passed begged Remandji to stop; but our fleet was bound for a village whose chief was called Agobi, the father-in-law of Remandji, and who had made friends with me. We at last reached his village.

Loud cheers from the villagers welcomed us. Several canoes were upset at the landing by being knocked against each other; but the Apingi swim like fish, and the suit of clothes they wore (their own skin) dried so quickly that a wetting was of very little moment to them.

There was a grand Apingi dance that night, and no sleep for me.

After two days spent at Agobi's village we began to ascend the river again, but the current was so swift that we hardly seemed to make any headway. There was a good deal of shouting, hollaing, and cursing in the Apingi language before we fairly left the shore. The banks of this noble stream, down to the water's edge, were a mass of verdure. I began to congratulate myself that there would be no capsizing, and that I was not going to take a bath in the river. Our canoe was, as I have said, ahead of all the others, when suddenly a canoe, which was crossing the river from the left bank, came close to us. We thought, however, that it would pass above our bow, but it was borne down by the current, and, before we could get out of the way, swept down upon us in spite of the shouts of Remandji and his man. The canoe had only an old woman in it. Bang! bang! and before I had time to say "Look out," both canoes were capsized, and there we were in the river.

Remandji was perfectly frantic, cursing the old woman while he was swimming. She did not in the least mind what he said, but swam off down stream like a buoy, shouting continually, "Where is my bunch of plantains? Give me back my plantains!" for I must say that, if we were angry at her, and blamed her for the accident, she was equally angry at us for the same reason, each thinking it was the other's fault.

The whole fleet was in great excitement, and Remandji was in a fearful rage at the idea of any one upsetting his moguizi. I was still in the water, holding on to the canoe as hard as I could, looking after the old woman, who soon reached the shore, and, climbing out at a bend of the river, waited for her capsized canoe to float along, which having secured, she got in and paddled off, full of complaints at losing her plantains, and, of course, blaming us for it. Remandji kept telling her all the time (I give you the literal translation, for the negroes do not mince words) to shut her mouth; but the more he told her to keep still, the more she talked.

As for me, I at last succeeded in reaching the shore, Remandji securing the canoe. Nothing was lost, and my gun was safe; it was not loaded, for which I was thankful.

It was a good thing that we had kept close to the banks of the river, for if we had capsized in the middle of the stream we should have gone a mile or two down the river before reaching the shore. I was not sorry when we got back to Remandji's village, and his people were very glad to see us return.

I do not know what these Apingis will think about me next. Remandji was a very intelligent fellow. As I am writing about him, I fancy I see his face and that I am talking to him. Remandji was not a very tall negro. He was white-headed, with a mild expression of countenance, very kind to his people, and respected by all his tribe. If there was any quarrel among them, they would come to him to settle it.

As you have seen, there was some fine hunting in his country. Leopards were somewhat plentiful in the forest, and one day I said to the king, "Remandji, I must go and hunt leopards, for I want their skins." He immediately asked, pointing to my coat, if I wanted a coat made of leopard's skin. I said no. Then he left me, and a little while after came back with a man, and said, "It is of no use for you to go into the jungle, for we want to see you all the time. Here is a man who has a big fetich, which enables him to kill all the leopards he wants without the fear of being killed by them." I burst out laughing. The man said, "Laugh, O spirit; but you will see."

The next morning, before starting, he came to show himself. When he made his appearance he began a most curious dance, talking sometimes very loud, at other times in a whisper, and making as many contortions as it is possible for a man to do. I could hardly recognize him. He did not look at all like the man of the day before. He was painted with ochre—half the body yellow, the other half red; one side of his face was red, the other white. On his head he had a covering made entirely of long feathers from the tails of strange birds. Round his neck and shoulders hung an iron chain, each link being about one inch long, and oval. To this chain was suspended the skin of an animal which I had never seen, called ndesha, a species of large wild-cat found in the forest. It was spotted somewhat like the skin of a leopard, but the ground part was reddish. The only portion that could be seen was that part near the tail, which hung down. In this skin was tied a wonderful fetich, which no other man possessed, and by which he was able, as I have said, to slay the leopards. The name of the man was Okabi. So I said, "Okabi, show me this monda." He replied that no one could see that monda, for if they did they would try to make one like it.

Round his waist he wore a belt made of a leopard's skin, which had been cut from the head, along the spine, to the tail. They believe that no spear can go through such belts. They are very much prized, each warrior placing great value upon his personal safety.

This leopard-charmer started quite alone, and I thought no more about him during the day.

In the evening I was seated on one of those little round Apingi stools, and Remandji and I were talking about the back country. I felt very much interested in the account he gave me of it, as he spoke of a tribe of people I had never seen, when lo! what did I see? Okabi, carrying on his back a dead leopard! I rubbed my eyes, thinking it was a mistake. No; it was Okabi himself, and a dead leopard.

How Okabi got the leopard I could not imagine, but surely he had it, and there was no mistake about it. He placed the leopard at my feet, saying, "Did I not tell you I had a fetich to kill leopards?" Remandji also

OKABI AND THE LEOPARD.

said, "Did I not tell you I had a man who had a big fetich to kill leopards?"

"I believe," said I to Remandji, "that when he promised to kill a leopard for me he had a trap set, and he knew that a leopard was in it. For," said I, "no man can make leopards come to him." "Oh yes," said Remandji, "there are men who have fetiches which have power to make game come to them."

I coaxed Okabi to show me his leopard fetich. He promised to do so the next day. He came, but I have very little doubt that he took something off from it he did not want me to see.

He entered my hut and then untied the skin, and after he spread it out I saw the contents which made the fetich. There were ashes of different plants, little pieces of wood, the small head of a young squirrel, claws of the wonderful guanionien, feathers of birds, bones of animals I could not recognize, bones of birds, dried intestines of animals, some dried brain of young chimpanzee, a very rare land-shell, scales of fishes, a little bit of scrapings from the skull of one of his ancestors. These were the things that made the leopards come to him.

"And if one of all these things you see," said he to me, "were missing, the fetich or monda would be good for nothing."

Time passed pleasantly in that fine country, and one day, as I was quietly reading my Bible outside of my hut, a crowd assembled and watched me with wondering eyes. I told them that when I read this book it taught me that God was the Great Spirit who had made the stars, the moon, the rivers, the mountains, and all the wild beasts, and every thing that was in the world.

Then I read some verses aloud to them. I told them that God said people must not worship that which they had made with their own hands, but any thing they wanted they must ask of him. They must love him. He said people must not tell lies—must not kill.

Presently I let the leaves of the book slip through my hands to show them how many there were. As the leaves slipped quickly from between my hand they made a slight noise, when, to my great surprise, as soon as they heard it they fled. In an instant the whole crowd, Remandji and all, had disappeared, with symptoms of the greatest terror. It was who should run the fastest. I called them back, but it was in vain. The louder I shouted, the faster they ran. The whole village was soon entirely deserted.

I shouted, "Remandji, come back—people, come back. I will do you no harm."

By-and-by I saw Remandji's face peeping from behind a plantain-tree. I called him, saying "that he and his people ought to be ashamed of themselves for leaving me alone in the village." At last they came back, when Remandji said, "O spirit! we ran away, for the noise made by what you held in your hand (meaning the Bible) was like that made by Ococoo, and we knew not what was coming next. We did not know that you and Ococoo could talk together." Ococoo is one of the chief spirits of the Apingi.

I told them it was all nonsense, and took the book again, but they begged me to let it alone.

In my frequent hunting-trips through the jungle, I found a great many palm-trees of the kind that yields the oil known as palm oil. I had never before seen such numbers of palms, all hanging full of ripe nuts. The Apingi eat these nuts. Their women come loaded every day with baskets full. They eat them roasted or boiled.

The oil is used for the ladies' toilets, either as cold cream for the skin or pomade for the hair. This cold cream is rather peculiar. The oil is mixed with clay, and they rub their bodies with this *clean and delightful mixture*. As a pomade, they sometimes put more than half a pound of it on their hair. Every few days they oil their heads, often mixing clay with the oil, and, as they never wash, and soap is unknown, the fragrance coming therefrom is not of the most odoriferous kind, and made me often wish that I had a cold, or could not smell.

These ladies wear charming little ear ornaments in the shape of rings three or four inches in diameter, the wire being often of the size of a lady's little finger. Of course the hole in the lobe of the ear is quite large. Their faces are tattooed all over, and, to crown the whole of the description, they have, as has before been observed, a beautiful mouth, ornamented in front by two rows of teeth filed to a sharp point.

They have a peculiar form of tattooed lines which is thought by them to be most beautiful. A broad stripe is drawn from the back of the neck along the shoulders, and across the breasts, meeting in an acute angle in the hollow of the chest. The flesh is raised at least two lines from the level of the skin. Other stripes are drawn in curves along the back, and from the breast down on the abdomen. The legs and arms are tattooed all over, and their faces are literally cut to pieces.

I never saw so much tattooing in any of the tribes I visited as among the Apingi. They seemed to like it; and when I reproached them for spoiling their bodies in such a manner, they replied, "Why, we think it is beautiful." And, pointing to my clothes, "Why do you wear garments?" said they. "These tattooings are like your garments; we think they are very fine."

Trouble loomed in the distance for me. The people insisted that I must get married. Remandji said that he must give me a housekeeper to keep my house and cook food for me. It was so; I must have a cook. The weather was hot and unpleasant, and it would be rather nice to have some one to attend to the kitchen. I smiled; it was a good idea. "Yes," I said, "I want a housekeeper."

Remandji brought me a lot of women. I chose the ugliest, whose pretty good likeness you have below, and installed her as my housekeeper, cook, and maid-of-all-work. For two or three days all went well, when, one fine morning, a deputation of men and women from a

MY HOUSEKEEPER.

neighboring village came to me, smiling and looking happy. They brought goats, fowls, and plantains; hailed me as their relative, and said that they came to ask for presents.

I confess that I lost my temper. I took a stick from my hut, the sight of which drove my would-be relatives and my housekeeper out of the village. They fled in the utmost consternation.

"Really," said I to myself, "these Apingi are a strange people."

Remandji laughed heartily at the adventurers, saying to them, "I told you not to go to the spirit, as he would get angry at you."

CHAPTER XXXI.

A GREAT CROWD OF STRANGERS.—I AM MADE A KING.— I REMAIN IN MY KINGDOM. — GOOD-BY TO THE YOUNG FOLKS.

The village was crowded with strangers once more. All the chiefs of the tribe had arrived. What did it all mean?

They had the wildest notions regarding me. I was the most wonderful of creatures—a mighty spirit. I could work wonders—turn wood into iron, leaves of trees into cloth, earth into beads, the waters of the Rembo Apingi into palm wine or plantain wine. I could make fire, the matches I lighted being proof of it.

What had that immense crowd come for? They had met to make me their king. A kendo, the insignia of chieftainship here, had been procured from the Shimba people, from whose country the kendo comes.

The drums beat early this morning; it seemed as if a fête-day was coming, for every one appeared joyous. I was quite unprepared for the ceremony that was to take place, for I knew nothing about it; no one had breathed a word concerning it to me. When the hour arrived I was called out of my hut. Wild shouts rang through the air as I made my appearance—"Yo! yo! yo!" The chiefs of the tribe, headed by Remandji, advanced toward me in line, each chief being armed with a spear, the heads of which they held pointed at me. In rear of the chiefs were hundreds of Apingi warriors, also armed with spears. Were they to spear me? They stopped, while the drummers beat their tam-tams furiously. Then Remandji, holding a kendo in his hand, came forward in the midst of the greatest excitement and wild shouts of "The moguizi is to be made our king! the moguizi is to be made our king!"

When Remandji stood about a yard from me a dead silence took place. The king advanced another step, and then with his right hand put the kendo on my left shoulder, saying, "You are the spirit whom we have never seen before. We are but poor people when we see you. You are one of those of whom we have heard, who came from nobody knows where, and whom we never expected to see. You are our king. We make you our king. Stay with us always, for we love you!" Whereupon shouts as wild as the country around came from the multitude. They shouted, "Spirit, we do not want you to go away—we want you forever!"

Immense quantities of palm wine, contained in calabashes, were drank, and a general jollification took place in the orthodox fashion of a coronation.

From that day, therefore, I may call myself Du Chaillu the First, King of the Apingi. Just fancy, I am an African king! Of all the wild castles I ever built when I was a boy, I never dreamed that I should one day be made king over a wild tribe of negroes dwelling in the mountains of Equatorial Africa.

I will remain in my kingdom for a while, and see every thing strange that there is in it. In the mean time, dear Young Folks, I bid you good-by, promising that, should you like to hear more of the country I have explored, I will, in another year, bring you back to the strange land where you and I have had so many adventures together.

www.ingramcontent.com/pod-product-compliance
Lightning Source LLC
Chambersburg PA
CBHW021344230426
43666CB00006B/407